HUMAN

Being Human in a World That Is Becoming Less Human

Technology is becoming more human.
The question is whether we are.

Justin Thomas

About this edition

Published by JTs Advisory Group LLC. Revised and expanded, October 2026.

This is narrative nonfiction supported by research and clearly identified illustrative fiction. The Rivera family and other unnamed scenes are fictional, not reported interviews. Hypothetical situations are introduced as such. Named people, historical events, and research findings are documented in the notes. The book does not invent dialogue or private thoughts for the subjects of reported cases.

The interpretive illustrations do not depict documented people or events. The manuscript has been developed with AI assistance and AI-generated editorial material.

This book offers social and ethical commentary, not individualized medical, legal, or mental-health advice. Research findings are bounded by their stated settings and dates. No claim is made that all people are becoming less humane, or that human dignity depends on any particular ability.

For the people still becoming

For the people who looked up.

And for those of us still learning how.

Contents

Contents

A Note to the Reader

There is a strange moment in a conversation with a capable machine when you stop thinking about the machine. You ask another question. You clarify what you meant. It responds with patience, sometimes more patience than you have received from a person that day. The exchange may help. It may also leave you with a question the system cannot settle for you: what, exactly, happened between us?

HUMAN begins there, in the space between what technology can do and what we make of it. Artificial intelligence can help people learn, communicate, create, and solve problems. It can also make consequential mistakes, conceal the choices of the organizations deploying it, and encourage habits we have not deliberately chosen. Its effects are not one story. Neither are we.

This is a book about ordinary people living through an extraordinary change. Some use AI constantly. Others rarely see it, yet encounter its consequences at work, at school, in public services, and in the information reaching their homes. No technical background or position of authority is required to belong in this conversation.

The title is a question about how we treat one another, not a claim that human beings are losing their humanity. A person who needs a device to speak is not less human. A tired parent who misses a question is not less human. Neither is someone unable to work, remember a name, or keep pace with a changing world. Dignity is not a prize awarded for winning a contest with a machine.

When these pages ask us to become more human, they ask us to become more humane: more able to recognize other lives as real, to remain answerable for our choices, and to make room for curiosity, care, and participation. Those qualities do not exhaust the meaning of humanity. They are qualities worth strengthening as our tools grow more powerful.

The Rivera family and the other unnamed scenes are fictional. They bring the questions into ordinary life; they are not reported interviews. Named people, historical events, and research findings are documented in the notes. No dialogue or private thought has been invented for the subjects of those reported cases.

The chapters widen from a conversation with a machine to the habits of a person, the life of a relationship, and the choices of societies whose circumstances differ greatly. The book does not ask everyone to fear the same things or want the same future. It asks how people with different needs might still recognize obligations to one another.

Research can help us see more clearly without settling every question. A result from one classroom or workplace is not a prediction for everyone. The notes identify the sources, dates, and limits behind the evidence; the judgments drawn from it remain open to examination.

There are no worksheets to complete here. There are people to consider, assumptions to test, and a question to carry into the world: if our tools become more capable, what would make our lives become better?

An Ordinary Tuesday

At 6:14 on a Tuesday evening, Maya Rivera stood at the kitchen counter separating cilantro leaves from their stems while her phone vibrated against a bowl of limes. She had been home from the hospital for eleven minutes. Her shoes were still on. A pale half-moon from her N95 mask remained pressed into the bridge of her nose.

"Can somebody get that?" she called.

Daniel was in the garage finishing a call with a supervisor from the distribution center. Eli, sixteen, sat three feet from the phone and did not look up. He had headphones on, although no music was playing. Nine-year-old Sofia was under the table retrieving a marker cap. In the living room, Daniel's mother, Rosa, watched a game show at a volume everyone pretended not to notice.

The phone stopped. Then it began again.

Maya wiped her hands and answered. It was the hospital. Someone had called out for the night shift. They were asking whether she could return.

"I just got home," she said, softly enough that the person on the other end might mistake it for information rather than refusal.

She looked toward the dining table. Five places had been set, though one fork was missing. Daniel came inside and saw her expression. He did not ask who was calling. He knew.

The request was reasonable. That was what made it hard. A colleague needed coverage, patients needed care, and Maya knew the pressure on the person making the call. She also knew that saying yes would mean leaving the table she had just come home to.

Maya said no. The word surprised her. It sounded almost rude in the kitchen.

They ate twenty minutes later. Eli kept his phone beside his thigh and checked it whenever he believed no one was watching. Sofia narrated a dispute from recess involving a jump rope and a girl named Brooklyn. Rosa complained that the tomatoes tasted like water. Daniel laughed so suddenly that Maya laughed too, although she had missed the sentence that caused it.

The rice was slightly undercooked. Rosa asked for salt. Halfway through dinner the hospital called someone else.

After dinner, Daniel cleared the plates while Maya found the missing fork under a school folder. Nothing about the evening suggested it would become a memory anyone kept.

What ordinary life is made of

We tend to notice ordinary life when something interrupts it. A loss can make a familiar voice feel irreplaceable. A move can make us miss a kitchen we once complained about. But loss should not have to do all our noticing for us.

There are also chances to notice while the people are still here. A child changes the way they tell a story. A parent starts asking for help with something they used to do easily. Someone says, "You seem busy," and stops talking. We may not be able to give every moment our full attention. We can learn to hear when a familiar explanation has started to hurt.

Attention has limits. Giving it to one thing usually means taking it from another. That is ordinary life, not a personal failure. The trouble begins when we stop noticing the choice and let whatever interrupts most often make it for us.

Employers, platforms, advertisers, newsrooms, and entertainment services all make claims on that attention. Many offer something worth having. Their needs do not disappear when ours are met, though. A feed can always supply another item. Work can usually supply another task. We need some way to decide when we have given enough.

We can know what is happening everywhere and miss what is happening beside us. We can preserve thousands of photographs and struggle to remember an afternoon. The danger is a life crowded with information whose ordinary pleasures and obligations barely receive our attention.

Maya could not make the hospital fully staffed by leaving dinner. She could not make every evening available to her family either. That Tuesday, she made a choice she could explain and stayed long enough to experience it.

AI brings more of these choices into reach. A recommendation system may help select what we see. A generative system may draft the message, explain the problem, or answer when nobody else is awake. These are different uses, with different effects. Not every screen or automated process is AI, but all can change where our attention goes and what we practice.

The chapters ahead ask what happens when an invitation to receive help becomes a habit of handing over the whole task. We can use an explanation without giving up curiosity. We can improve a message without surrendering what we mean. We can accept a recommendation and still be responsible for the decision. The distinction becomes real in what we do after the answer arrives.

Yet a household is not an island. Maya's ability to stay at dinner depended partly on a staffing decision made elsewhere. Daniel's remaining work depended on a schedule he had not designed alone. Their children would encounter educational technologies chosen by adults they had never met. The shape of their evening belonged both to them and to the systems around them.

That is why this story cannot end with advice to put a phone away. A person can make a thoughtful choice and still live inside an arrangement that makes the same choice difficult tomorrow. A society can praise presence while rewarding permanent availability. It can celebrate care while making the people who provide it struggle to pay their bills.

AI enters these arrangements with a promise: more can be done. More messages can be answered, more patterns recognized, more lessons adapted, more plans considered. Sometimes that promise will be fulfilled in ways that make life genuinely better. Sometimes the newly available capacity will simply become a newly expected pace. Someone will decide which.

The future will be built partly in laboratories, but it will arrive in places like this kitchen. It will arrive as a scheduling change, an explanation a child trusts, a voice a lonely person returns to, or a form that accepts no account of an unusual life. It will also arrive as help: a sentence finally understood, a task made possible, time recovered after an exhausting day.

We need a language large enough to describe both. We need to understand the technology without letting technology become the only measure of what matters. Most of all, we need to ask what kind of life the growing power is supposed to serve.

PART 1

The Machine in the Mirror

What is AI becoming, and why does it feel so human?

CHAPTER 01

The Day Intelligence Moved

The answer on the screen

Imagine a woman trying to understand a letter that has arrived from a public agency. The letter is written in the language she uses at work, but not the language in which she thinks when she is frightened. It refers to an earlier notice she does not remember receiving. There is a date near the bottom, a paragraph of exceptions, and a helpline that stops taking calls before her shift ends.

She asks an AI system to explain it. In seconds, the letter becomes plain language. The system identifies the deadline, separates the requested documents from the background information, and suggests questions she might ask. Something that felt like a wall now resembles a set of steps.

That help can be real. It can also be incomplete. Perhaps the image she uploaded cuts off a line. Perhaps the system confuses two procedures. Perhaps the rule has changed since the material it relies on was produced. A useful explanation does not establish that every detail is correct. Yet the answer arrives in the same calm voice whether its foundation is strong or weak.

The woman is not foolish if she feels relief. Relief is one reason the technology matters. The question is whether the surrounding service gives her a reliable way to check what matters, correct an error, and speak to someone empowered to help. The quality of her experience depends on more than the quality of a sentence.

This hypothetical letter contains much of the larger story. AI can lower a barrier that should not have been so high in the first place. It can also become a new barrier if an institution decides the availability of an automated explanation makes accountable human assistance unnecessary. The same apparent improvement can lead toward participation or toward another form of exclusion.

We cannot judge which by asking only whether the answer looks impressive. We must follow what happens next.

The shock of a machine doing something once associated with human intelligence is not new. Earlier encounters can help us see what changes when a capability arrives, and what does not. Before the familiar conversation box came games in which the rules were clear and the result could not be explained away.

In May 1997, Garry Kasparov faced IBM's Deep Blue in a six-game rematch in New York. The reigning world chess champion had won their first match the previous year. This time, a human operator moved the machine's pieces. The opponent whose decisions he carried had no face to study and no nerves to betray it.

Deep Blue won the final game and the match, three and a half to two and a half. It was the first computer system to defeat a reigning world chess champion in a match under standard tournament controls. The result mattered beyond chess because the game had long served as shorthand for human intellect.

Deep Blue did not play chess as Kasparov did. It evaluated as many as two hundred million positions per second, combining immense computational force with evaluation methods and knowledge shaped by its engineers and chess experts. It did not fear defeat or savor victory. It did not know that cameras were watching. Yet on the narrow field that mattered that week, those absences did not prevent it from winning. [1]

New tools can unsettle familiar ways of understanding our abilities. A task that took years to master may become easier or less valuable in the market. That can be useful to the person needing the task done and painful to the person whose livelihood depended on doing it.

Chess carried a special burden because it seemed to require not only calculation but intuition, imagination, and style. The board was finite; the meanings placed upon it were not. A champion did more than choose legal moves. He perceived patterns invisible to weaker players and made judgments under uncertainty. If a machine could win there, people wondered, what precisely had it demonstrated?

Deep Blue could win at chess without possessing the range of abilities we expect from a person. That matters because success on one task does not settle what a system understands, what else it can do, or what authority we should give it.

Nineteen years after Deep Blue, another board became the site of another contest. Go is played with black and white stones on a grid. Its simple rules allow an enormous range of possible play. In March 2016, Google DeepMind's AlphaGo faced Lee Sedol in Seoul. Lee had won eighteen world titles and was one of the world's leading players.

During the second game, AlphaGo played Move 37, a choice commentators initially questioned. DeepMind later described it as having roughly a one-in-ten-thousand chance of selection by a human player. Its strategic value became clearer as the game continued. Lee lost.

The moment disturbed a comforting explanation of machine superiority. Deep Blue could be described as brute force: a machine calculating farther and faster. Move 37 looked different. It appeared unconventional, strategic, even creative. Lee later said that seeing it changed his understanding of the machine. The word *creative* had crossed the table.

Lee won the fourth game, the only human victory of the five-game match. His unexpected Move 78 became one of its defining moments. The result did not establish a permanent human advantage. It showed that the stronger system could still fail in a position that mattered. [2]

A tool can change a field without ending it. Chess and Go continued after these defeats. The harder question is what participation in a changed field requires, and who can afford the transition. The fact that a field survives offers little comfort to a particular person losing their place in it.

What capability does and does not tell us

AI is a broad name for systems built to perform tasks associated with intelligence. The label covers different designs and uses. A system that detects a pattern in an image, one that recommends a video, and one that generates a conversation should not be treated as interchangeable. Their errors differ. So do the questions we need to ask about them.

Generative systems produce new text, images, audio, or other material in response to instructions and context. In language models, training develops patterns that support the production of sequences of text. Further training and system design shape how the model follows instructions, interacts with tools, and handles particular requests. None of this makes every answer a verified retrieval from a library. A plausible continuation can include a statement that is false.

That distinction is easy to say and difficult to feel. A search result usually announces that other people have said something. A conversational answer may sound as though somebody has already considered the question and reached a conclusion. The form compresses the uncertainty. It can make the distance between asking and believing feel shorter than the work of verification deserves.

The responsible response is not to dismiss everything generated as meaningless. A translation may be useful. A draft may give someone the words they were struggling to find. A model may identify a pattern a person missed. Treating those benefits as unreal would prevent us from understanding why people adopt the tools. But usefulness on one task does not grant authority on every task.

A system might explain a familiar concept clearly and still fail on a subtle variation. It might summarize a document well while overlooking the qualification that changes its meaning. It might succeed when the relevant evidence is placed directly in front of it and fail when asked to supply evidence from memory-like generation. The practical unit of trust is the task in its context, not the general charm of the interface. [3]

People are inconsistent too. A doctor can be an excellent diagnostician and a poor listener. A teacher can know a subject and misunderstand a child. Human fallibility is not an argument for abandoning standards for AI. It is a reason to build standards around consequences rather than around allegiance to either humans or machines.

When the cost of error is low, experimentation may be easy to justify. A mistaken restaurant suggestion wastes a few minutes. When the cost is serious, the arrangement needs stronger safeguards. A medical decision, a legal deadline, or a change to someone's access to housing cannot be treated as a casual brainstorming session. The language on the screen may look equally polished in all of these situations. The stakes do not.

The machine that acts

The relationship changes again when an AI system can do more than answer. Connected to tools, it may search, retrieve records, draft a message, modify a document, or carry out steps in a workflow. Some systems follow a sequence designed in advance; others choose intermediate steps within a wider task. Their capabilities depend on the tools, permissions, and constraints around them. A useful explanation of these differences appears in Anthropic's account of workflows and agents. [4]

The difference between suggesting and doing is not a minor interface detail. A draft can be rejected before anyone sees it. A sent message has already entered another person's life. A proposed appointment can be checked. A canceled appointment may have to be recovered. The moment an answer becomes an action, questions about consent, authority, and reversibility become immediate.

Consider an assistant arranging a trip for a family. The fastest itinerary might include a connection the grandmother cannot manage. The lowest price might exclude a change option the family needs. A system can optimize what it has been told to optimize while failing to understand what the family did not know it needed to say. The problem is not necessarily a computational error. It can be a poor account of the purpose.

Delegation has always required communication. We explain, correct, and revise arrangements with other people. But a person helping us may recognize the need to ask about something outside the stated task. Whether an automated system reliably does that must be tested, not assumed from its conversational confidence. The user also needs to know which actions are being considered, which have occurred, and which still require approval.

There is an ethical difference between an assistant that enlarges our ability to act and one that quietly acts beyond our understanding. Both may be described as convenient. Only one leaves the person meaningfully in charge. Meaningful control does not require approving every keystroke; it requires a comprehensible boundary between what has been delegated and what has not.

For someone overwhelmed by paperwork, a well-designed assistant might restore agency. For someone whose employer mandates a system without explanation or recourse, the same word, assistance, may describe a loss of agency. We should be suspicious of accounts that discuss the technology without discussing who gets to choose its role.

Fifteen percent in one workplace

In a study published in 2025, Erik Brynjolfsson, Danielle Li, and Lindsey Raymond examined an AI assistant used by 5,172 customer-support agents. Access increased the number of issues resolved per hour by fifteen percent on average. Less experienced and lower-skilled workers benefited most; gains were much smaller for their more experienced, higher-skilled colleagues.

The researchers also found evidence of learning and improvements in the experience of work. This was one deployment, not a productivity rate every organization can expect. And the performance measure cannot decide how the gain should be used. Shorter waits, better training, less pressure, and higher targets are different choices. [5]

What it means to become more human

The title's provocation needs care. Technology can become more humanlike in its expression, responsiveness, or outward behavior. That does not settle questions about subjective experience. Whether and under what conditions an artificial system could have such experience remains disputed. This book does not use a moving exchange as proof of an inner life, or a technical description as a complete answer to a philosophical question.

It is a mistake to defend humanity by continually moving a competitive boundary. First we say machines cannot calculate as we do, then that they cannot play as we do, then that they cannot write or create as we do. Every advance can feel like an invasion of the territory we used to prove our worth. But worth was never safely located there.

What matters is not preserving a task that no machine may ever perform. It is deciding what kinds of relationships and obligations should organize life among people. A machine may help write an apology. The person who caused harm still has to accept responsibility. A system may suggest a fair arrangement. The people living under it still deserve a voice. A tool may make care easier. Someone must still choose to provide it.

This does not mean responsibility rests only on the individual user. Designers choose defaults. Employers choose expectations. Public institutions choose procedures. Families and communities develop norms. A person's choices are made inside these arrangements, sometimes freely and sometimes under considerable pressure. Becoming more humane requires changing the arrangements as well as improving ourselves.

There is no guarantee that greater technical capability will produce greater kindness. Neither is there a law that it must diminish it. The relationship is a task, not a destiny. Understanding that gives us something more useful than either panic or surrender: a reason to participate in deciding what the tools are for.

When we say this technology is evolving, we are describing changes in systems people build, train, test, and deploy. We are not describing a child growing up. The word should not hide the choices behind the product: what it is designed to do, whose needs it serves, and what its makers allow it to do without us.

What changes in us

Our side of the relationship changes less visibly. We may begin asking for an answer sooner, attempting something we once avoided, or expecting other people to respond with the speed and patience of a machine. Here, human evolution means the ways we adapt in daily life, not a claim that our biology is changing to match a software release.

We should leave room for what we do not yet know. A useful afternoon does not establish a lasting benefit. A difficult encounter does not establish inevitable decline. We can notice an effect in our own lives without turning it into a verdict on every human being. The question is worth returning to: what am I becoming more able to do, and what am I no longer practicing?

The aim is not to keep everything as it was. Some changes deserve to be welcomed. It is to understand enough of the relationship to participate in shaping it. That includes asking whether a new capability leaves people with more room to learn and live, not only whether it gets a task done faster.

The woman with the agency letter does not need her assistant to be human. She needs its help to reach another person. That difference will matter long after the next, more impressive answer arrives.

CHAPTER 02

A Voice That Sounds Like Ours

The message arrived after dinner. In this imagined household, a father had been waiting for his adult daughter to respond after an awkward conversation the previous weekend. He had offered advice when she wanted him to listen. She had accused him of treating every difficult feeling as a problem to solve. Neither had quite apologized.

Now there were three paragraphs on his phone. They were generous, clear, and unusually composed. She acknowledged his intentions without withdrawing her complaint. She described what she needed. She ended by saying she wanted them to find a better way to talk.

He read the message twice. Then he called her.

"Did you write this?"

She hesitated. "I knew what I wanted to say. I used something to help."

He felt the relief of the message turn into suspicion. Had the words meant less because a machine helped arrange them? She felt the risk she had taken disappear beneath a new accusation. She had spent an hour changing the draft, removing sentences that were not true, and adding the part she had been afraid to say. None of that effort was visible to him.

The exchange could have become an argument about cheating. Instead, after a silence, he asked a more useful question.

"Which part was hardest to tell me?"

She did not need help answering that.

The work behind the words

It is tempting to sort communication into two categories: authentic human expression and artificial substitution. Actual use is less tidy. A person may use assistance to escape the work of reflection. Another may use it to undertake a conversation they would otherwise avoid. The same feature can serve different intentions and produce different effects.

People have always received help expressing themselves. A friend rehearses an important conversation with us. An editor improves a sentence. A translator carries meaning between languages. A speech device makes expression possible. Assistance does not automatically empty the resulting words of sincerity.

The important questions concern the relationship between the words and the person using them. Do they recognize the meaning? Have they considered the promises? Are they willing to answer for what has been said? Can the recipient ask a question that was not anticipated in the draft and receive a person in reply?

A perfectly written apology can be an evasion if its sender has no intention of changing. A clumsy apology can be sincere and still need clarification. Fluency is not a reliable measure of either. What happens after the message matters: the call returned, the behavior altered, the disagreement endured without withdrawing care.

For someone anxious about language, AI assistance may offer a bridge into that work. For someone determined to avoid responsibility, it may provide a more attractive place to hide. We should judge the practice by what it enables in the relationship, not by the mere presence or absence of a tool.

Disclosure also depends on context. A recipient may care deeply whether a wedding vow, a condolence, a recommendation, or a professional judgment has been generated or substantially assisted. Expectations differ, and some institutions impose explicit rules. Where the origin changes how another person would understand the communication, concealment can become part of the harm. The ethical question is not solved by insisting that everybody uses tools.

When a machine sounds compassionate

In a 2023 study, researchers compared physicians' responses to 195 questions from an online forum with answers generated by a chatbot. Healthcare evaluators preferred the chatbot responses in 78.6 percent of evaluations and rated them higher for empathy. The chatbot answers were generally longer. The study assessed written responses, not the quality of an ongoing clinical relationship, patient outcomes, or a machine's capacity to feel. It should not be read as a verdict that AI is a better doctor. [6]

The finding still asks an uncomfortable question. Why might language produced by a machine feel more considerate than language from a person whose work is to help? One possible response is to celebrate the system. Another is to defend the people. A more useful response considers the conditions under which care is being expressed.

Imagine a clinician answering messages between appointments, another shift running late, a family waiting outside an examination room. A brief answer may reflect limited time rather than limited concern. That does not make a patient's experience of being dismissed unreal. It makes the problem larger than the character of either participant.

An institution could use AI to help a clinician draft a fuller explanation, with the clinician checking its accuracy and adapting it to the patient. It could also use AI as a reason to increase the number of messages each clinician must handle, leaving even less time for difficult conversations. The same technical capability could support care or intensify the conditions that undermine it.

This is the difference between making compassion easier to express and making the appearance of compassion cheaper to deliver. The two can look similar on a screen. They diverge when the person needs clarification, judgment, continuity, or an action that an agreeable sentence cannot perform.

We should welcome better explanations. People deserve to understand what is happening to them. But a warm response must not be allowed to close the door on the person who still needs help. The point of language that sounds caring should be to improve care, not to replace the obligation to provide it.

The invitation of a voice

A voice brings more than words. A pause can suggest attention. A change in pace can suggest concern. A remembered preference can suggest familiarity. When these features appear in an interface, they can make interaction easier and more accessible. They can also encourage us to interpret a service through expectations developed in relationships with people.

The inference is understandable. We encounter most responsive language in human settings. We have learned to pay attention to signs that somebody understands, cares, or remembers. A convincing imitation of those signs can affect us even while we know what produced it. Knowing how a film is made does not stop us from crying at it.

The emotion is real. The interpretation still deserves examination. A person may feel comforted by a generated response without the system occupying the same kind of relationship as a friend. We do not have to ridicule the comfort to ask what else is happening: what data is retained, what the service rewards, what the user expects, and what alternatives are available.

An interface can be friendly without suggesting that it has needs the user must meet. It can remember a preference without making its commercial relationship disappear. It can acknowledge a difficult feeling without claiming privileged knowledge of a person's life. The design choices matter because they shape the meaning users are invited to make.

Consider the difference between a tool that helps someone rehearse a conversation and one that continually reassures them that people who disagree are unworthy of their attention. The first may make participation easier. The second may make retreat more comfortable.

Friendliness is not the problem. The problem is a relationship whose apparent meaning obscures its actual conditions. People should not have to choose between a cold, unusable tool and a warm interface that invites misunderstanding about what is on the other side.

The value of an imperfect reply

There is a particular kind of trust in hearing someone say, "I don't know how to answer that yet." The sentence offers little immediate satisfaction. It may be disappointing. But it leaves room for a person to think rather than perform certainty.

People do not always use that room well. We can delay because we are avoiding, and we can dress indifference as thoughtful restraint. Still, the existence of a pause gives a relationship something that continuous fluency can obscure: evidence that an answer may require work, limits, and a choice about what can honestly be promised.

As generated language becomes more available, human communication may be tempted toward constant polish. The temptation will not be limited to formal writing. A person may begin to distrust their own unfinished sentences, their ordinary humor, or their inability to respond immediately with the perfect reassurance. Everyday talk could start to feel like a poor version of its edited alternative.

That would be an unfortunate standard for intimacy. The people close to us do not only need our most effective presentation. They sometimes need to see us thinking, changing our minds, and admitting that we have misunderstood. A relationship can survive awkward language more easily than a persistent absence of genuine participation.

The father and daughter could have remained trapped in a question of authorship. Who made the paragraphs? That question mattered, but it was not the only one. Once he asked which part was hardest, she explained that she wanted to tell him about her life without preparing a defense of every decision. He began to explain why he worried. She interrupted. He tried again.

Nothing in the call was as smooth as the message. The conversation was more important.

CHAPTER 03

Who Answers for the Decision

Imagine a wildfire moving faster than expected. In the emergency center, maps refreshed, wind models changed, and colored zones widened across neighborhoods. The system could estimate where the fire might travel. It could not decide when uncertainty had become dangerous enough to order thousands of people from their homes.

Evacuate too early and the roads might clog, resources scatter, and public trust erode. Wait too long and the cost would be measured in lives. Every option contained risk. The incident commander listened to meteorologists, firefighters, police, and local officials. Then she made the call.

Judgment is needed when evidence leaves more than one defensible choice. It means explaining what we know, what remains uncertain, and why we are acting now. Confidence alone is not enough. Waiting also has consequences.

Artificial intelligence can improve the field on which judgment operates. Reliable prediction, pattern recognition, and simulation may reveal consequences a human team could otherwise miss. Where the evidence supports a tool and the safeguards fit the stakes, refusing its help can carry risks too.

The danger lies in confusing the recommendation with the decision. A model optimizes an objective selected by people. If the objective is incomplete, the answer may be precise and wrong in the way that matters. A hospital can minimize waiting time while making frightened patients feel processed. A school can maximize test performance while diminishing curiosity. A company can maximize output while destroying the conditions under which people remain well enough to produce it.

Judgment asks questions the objective excludes. Who bears the risk? Which value will be sacrificed? What precedent does this create? If everyone follows this rule, what kind of institution remains? What would I be willing to explain face-to-face to the person harmed?

We can learn from a decision without pretending the outcome was inevitable. Which part depended on evidence? Which part depended on what we hoped would happen? Looking back honestly helps us make the next choice with a clearer understanding of our own habits.

The evacuation order went out. The fire later turned. Some residents complained about the hours away from home; others were relieved that officials had not waited for certainty.

The commander reviewed the decision afterward with the information available when she made it. A favorable outcome did not prove every assumption sound, just as an unpopular order did not prove the risk unreal. She had to learn without pretending she had known how the fire would move.

What did you ask it to optimize?

A woman considering a new job asked an AI assistant which offer was better. She supplied the salaries, titles, and job descriptions. The comparison was thorough. It also left out the part she had barely admitted to herself: she wanted fewer evenings away from her father.

She had framed "better" as a career question, then treated the answer as though it had considered her whole life. When she added the travel and schedule, the comparison changed. She checked those details directly with the employers. A tidy table had made uncertain assumptions look settled.

The tool helped her see the tradeoffs once she named them. It could not decide what an evening with her father was worth to her. She still had to choose, including the possibility of regretting part of either choice.

There are two checks before a consequential decision: whether the information is reliable, and whether the goal is the one you actually want. A system can make a mistake about the facts. It can also organize the facts correctly around a goal you have described too narrowly.

Ask what the answer depends on. Which statements came from you? Which need confirmation elsewhere? What would change the recommendation? If health, money, rights, or safety are at stake, use the response to prepare for qualified advice and consult authoritative information. The system's explanation of its own confidence is not an independent check.

The U.S. National Institute of Standards and Technology's 2024 generative AI risk profile identifies false but confidently expressed output, privacy risks, and inappropriate reliance on AI among the risks to manage. Those concerns are reasons to match our trust to the task, rather than use the same level of scrutiny for a dinner idea and a decision someone will have to live with. [3]

Responsibility also means being willing to revise the decision when reality changes. Keep track of the important assumption, not every sentence of the conversation. If the assumption proves wrong, reconsider the choice. "The AI recommended it" explains how an option reached us; it does not finish our account of why we accepted it.

The person who receives the answer

An automated decision has two audiences. One sees the system's performance across a population. The other sees the decision that has arrived in their own life. A process can look efficient to the first audience while being impossible to understand from the position of the second.

Consider a fictional applicant whose request for a service has been rejected. The message is polite. It explains that the application does not meet the criteria. There is a link to general information and another to a form that asks the same questions again. Nothing identifies which part of the application caused the result.

The applicant has made an unusual but legitimate arrangement to care for a relative. The form does not contain the right category. Each attempt to describe it becomes a selection that is almost true. By the time the application reaches the decision system, the person has already been translated into inaccurate terms.

The resulting problem cannot be solved solely by making the model more accurate on the existing fields. Someone has to recognize that the fields are inadequate. Someone needs authority to hear a fact that the process has no place to store. A system that only permits correction within its own categories may make a person repeat the same misrepresentation indefinitely.

A person affected by a decision needs more than an explanation that a system produced it. They need a way to supply missing information, question a mistake, and reach someone able to act on what they say.

An explanation is not an appeal

There are several things people may need after a consequential decision. They may need to know what happened. They may need to correct a factual error. They may want a rule reconsidered, or an exception evaluated. They may need a temporary arrangement while a dispute is reviewed. These are different needs.

A system can produce an elegant explanation while offering no meaningful remedy. It can explain why a rule was applied without asking whether the rule belongs in the situation. It can direct someone to an appeal channel whose reviewers lack time or authority. The appearance of transparency should not be confused with the power to correct a wrong.

For the institution, an appeal is sometimes experienced as friction. For the person affected, it may be the first moment the institution encounters the reality of their circumstances. Treating every objection as an obstacle to efficiency risks eliminating one of the ways a system learns where its assumptions fail.

Human review is not automatically sufficient. A reviewer can accept a system's recommendation without examining it. A signature can become ceremonial. The phrase human in the loop matters only if the human has enough information, time, independence, and authority to change the result when the result is wrong.

Responsibility also cannot be pushed endlessly down the chain. The user blames the model. The institution blames the vendor. The vendor points to the customer's settings. Each explanation may contain a fact, yet the injured person is still left without anyone willing to repair the consequence. An accountable arrangement identifies responsibilities before the error occurs.

What we choose to count

Measurement helps people coordinate. A hospital cannot run only on good intentions. A school needs ways to understand whether students are learning. A transport system needs to know whether buses arrive. Rejecting measurement because it is incomplete would make many essential services harder to provide.

The danger lies in allowing a measure to replace the purpose it was meant to serve. A fast appointment is useful if the patient receives appropriate care. Speed alone cannot tell us whether a concern was heard. A higher completion rate may indicate accessible teaching or assignments made easier without corresponding understanding. We need the measure and an account of what it leaves out.

Suppose a service is rewarded for reducing the number of people who contact support. It might achieve that by making its product easier to use. It might also achieve it by making contact more difficult. Without attention to the experience behind the number, the same metric can describe improvement or abandonment.

A service can look efficient while people quietly give up. Counting completed transactions will not reveal those who could not finish one. Their absence from the dashboard is part of the result, not evidence that the problem has gone away.

Shared responsibility without helplessness

When responsibility is distributed, people can feel that they possess too little influence to matter. A worker did not select the system. A parent did not write the school policy. A patient cannot redesign the appointment process while waiting for a diagnosis. It would be cruel to make every person responsible for repairing every institution they encounter.

Limited influence does not mean that only the people building the technology have a legitimate voice. The obligation remains: do not make other people live under your decision while denying them any account of it. A powerful system makes the consequences of ignoring that obligation easier to scale.

In the fictional application, a useful change might be modest: a reviewer who can read the explanation, ask one additional question, and correct the record. To an organization, that may look like an exception. To the person waiting, it is the difference between being processed and being understood.

What Entered the House

Three missed calls

The first call from the school arrived while Daniel was standing beneath a conveyor motor listening to a mechanic explain why a thirty-dollar bearing had stopped a line worth forty thousand dollars an hour. He saw the number, recognized it, and let the phone return to his pocket.

The second call came during the repair. The third came after the line restarted.

By then the message was waiting: *This is the counselor at West Mesa. Eli is safe. Please call us as soon as you can.*

Daniel stopped walking and read the message again.

Daniel called. The counselor said Eli had left chemistry class unable to breathe. His hands had gone numb. He believed he was dying. A teacher found him sitting against a locker and walked him to the counseling office.

"Was he using something?" Daniel asked.

There was a pause. "It may have been a panic attack. We've asked the school nurse to assess him. Because this is new, he needs medical follow-up too."

Daniel had heard the phrase before. He associated it with celebrities, airport terminals, and people who described their feelings more confidently than he did. In his family, fear had always been translated into action: work harder, drive faster, check the locks, say less.

At school, Eli sat beneath a poster about resilience. He looked embarrassed rather than ill.

"I'm fine now," he said.

Daniel nearly answered, *Good.* The word would have closed the subject and restored the shape of the day. Instead he sat in the chair beside him.

"What did it feel like?"

Eli looked at the counselor, then at his father. "Like my body knew something terrible that I didn't."

On the drive home, Daniel resisted every solution that appeared in his mind. Exercise. Less phone. Better sleep. A schedule. A speech about perspective. Some of those things might eventually help. None answered the question Eli had actually asked: would his father remain near him when the fear made no sense?

At a red light, Daniel said, "It happened to me once."

He had never told anyone. He was twenty-two, newly married, sitting in a truck outside a job interview. His heart began striking his ribs. He drove away before the interview and told Maya the company had canceled.

Eli turned toward him. "What did you do?"

"Pretended it didn't happen for twenty years."

The light changed. A horn sounded behind them.

At home, Daniel told Maya what he had said. The canceled interview was news to her too. They had another conversation to have.

The blue dot

Eli's first thought every morning was not a sentence. It was a blue dot.

The dot meant something had happened while he was asleep. Someone had replied, reacted, posted, invited, excluded, won, failed, broken up, looked incredible, looked ridiculous, or become briefly important. The dot made no claim that the news would matter by breakfast. It only promised that he was behind.

He reached for the phone before his eyes had adjusted to the room. By the time his feet touched the floor, he had already encountered a war, a joke, three bodies more muscular than his, a classmate's vacation, an advertisement for shoes he had searched once, and a video of a stranger crying in a parked car. He felt informed, entertained, envious, amused, and vaguely guilty before brushing his teeth.

At school, his English teacher placed a paperback on every desk. "Phones in the caddy," she said.

The class groaned. Eli slid his phone into slot seventeen. For the first ten minutes, he kept looking toward it. He reread one paragraph four times. Around him, chairs squeaked. Someone coughed. The clock made a sound he had never noticed before.

Then the book opened.

Not dramatically. There was no revelation. He simply stopped wondering what had happened elsewhere. A character entered a room carrying news she did not know how to deliver, and Eli followed her. Twenty-three minutes disappeared without asking to be filled.

When the bell rang, the class rushed the caddy. Eli checked the blue dot. Twelve notifications waited. Eleven meant nothing. The twelfth was a message from his father: *Can you help Grandma with her phone after school?*

He almost typed *busy*. Instead he wrote *sure*.

That afternoon Rosa handed him her phone and said it had lost the photographs. They were not lost; she had changed a setting. As he restored the gallery, he found hundreds of images she had never shown anyone: Daniel as a boy asleep across two kitchen chairs, Maya holding newborn Sofia, Eli missing his front teeth, Rosa's late husband standing beside a truck with one hand raised against the sun.

"Send me that one," Eli said.

Rosa looked at the photograph. "He hated having his picture taken."

Rosa kept finding photographs she wanted to explain. Eli missed the start of a game with his friends. Before he left, he sent himself three pictures and asked if they could look at the rest another day.

PART 2

What Is Happening to Us

While we teach machines, what are our tools teaching us?

CHAPTER 04

The Merchants of Attention

The young woman refreshed the screen again. The number had risen. It told her how many people had watched yesterday's video. She kept looking for what it said about her.

She created videos for a living, though "created" failed to capture the breadth of the job. She watched trends, tested openings, studied retention graphs, answered comments, negotiated with brands, and fed the machine with the regularity it rewarded. Some days the work felt playful and improbable. She had built an audience larger than the population of the town where she grew up. Other days she felt like a tenant living inside a house whose walls changed whenever she learned the floor plan.

When a video performed well, the graph rose like a promise. When it failed, she searched herself for the defect. Had she become boring? Had the lighting changed? Was the subject wrong, her face wrong, her life insufficiently alive? The platform offered data with exquisite precision and almost no wisdom. It could tell her when viewers left. It could not tell her when she should.

Attention has always been valuable. Orators competed for it in public squares; newspapers sold it to advertisers; radio and television organized evenings around it. What changed was not the existence of the marketplace but its intimacy, scale, and speed. The auction moved into our pockets. Measurement became continuous. The same device that carries our family photographs and private messages also hosts an industrial contest to influence what we notice next.

Every pause, swipe, replay, and purchase can become information used to decide what appears next. A service does not have to understand why something matters to us to learn that we keep returning to it. That difference matters when the behavior being rewarded is one we are trying to change.

This is not a conspiracy. It is a business model working as designed. Many of the people who build these products are thoughtful, decent, and alert to their risks. The services themselves can educate, delight, organize, reveal injustice, sustain small businesses, and connect the isolated. The moral complexity is real. So is the economic fact: when a service is free, human attention often helps pay the bill.

An endless feed removes the stopping point that a last page or closing time provides. We have to supply one ourselves. That sounds easy until we notice how often one more item turns into twenty minutes we meant to spend elsewhere.

The cost is not merely lost time. It is the fragmentation of intention. A person reaches for a phone to check the weather and returns twenty minutes later carrying outrage from a stranger, envy from an acquaintance, and a vague sense that everyone else is living more vividly. The original purpose disappears. This is what makes the experience so difficult to describe: we were active the entire time, yet afterward it can feel as though something happened to us.

Attention determines more than what we consume. It shapes what becomes available to thought. A mind repeatedly trained to expect novelty may struggle with the slow middle of a book, the silence required for reflection, or the unedited pace of another person's story. Deep attention has always required protection, but we now ask individuals to defend it against systems tested by armies of designers and optimized through oceans of behavioral data. Calling this a simple failure of discipline mistakes the scale of the contest.

Responsibility is shared, but it is not evenly distributed. A company can change a default for millions of people. A person can change a setting, remove an app, or decide where a phone lives at night. Those are different kinds of power. We should use the choices we have without pretending they cancel the obligations of the people designing the service.

The creator began taking walks without her phone. At first she experienced phantom emergencies. What if a client called? What if inspiration arrived without a camera? What if something happened and she could not prove she had seen it? She noticed how often her mind composed captions for things before it had experienced them. A dog running through leaves became an angle. Light on a brick wall became a post. Her life had acquired a second audience that followed her even when she was alone.

Over time, the walks lengthened. She recognized houses, trees, a man watering his front garden. The work still required her phone, and she still checked the numbers. But the walk had become a part of the day she did not have to turn into a performance.

The life selected for us

Imagine opening a service to answer a small question about repairing a chair. The first demonstration is useful. The second shows a more elegant method. The third reveals that the chair is part of a style you had never noticed. Soon there are rooms, then houses, then people apparently living inside the kind of life your own room has begun to lack.

Nothing especially sinister has happened. Nobody forced you to stay. You may even have enjoyed the journey. Yet the original purpose has changed without a clear moment of decision. You came to repair something you owned. You leave with a new dissatisfaction about what you do not own.

An afternoon can disappear this way without a single decision to surrender it. Each item makes the next one easy. The chair remains unrepaired because nothing on the screen ever quite says that we are finished.

AI can make such arrangements more responsive. That responsiveness may help someone find material they genuinely value. It can also make a commercial objective feel remarkably personal. An invitation that fits our interests can be harder to recognize as an invitation serving someone else's interests too.

Personalization is not inherently hostile to agency. The important question is whether it helps us pursue a purpose we can recognize, or keeps revising the purpose in ways we barely notice. A useful system can explain and expose choices. A less accountable one can treat our continued involvement as sufficient proof that it is helping.

Wanting and choosing

We often speak as though preference were a fixed object waiting to be discovered. In ordinary life, preference can develop through exposure. A friend introduces music we learn to love. A teacher reveals a subject we never expected to care about. A conversation changes what we believe is possible. Being influenced is part of being alive with other people.

The moral question is not whether influence occurs. It is how influence is exercised and what opportunities we have to understand or resist it. A friend may recommend a book because they think it will matter to us. A seller may recommend the same book because a sale matters to them. Both recommendations could be useful. Their motives still deserve to be distinguishable.

A system that anticipates what will keep us involved does not necessarily know what we would endorse after reflection. The thing that captures us when we are tired may not be the thing we want our evenings to become. The purchase that relieves discomfort for ten minutes may not address the discomfort. A recommendation can fit an immediate impulse while missing a larger intention.

That gap should not become another reason to despise ourselves. Human wanting has always been complicated. The challenge is to make room for the slower preferences that are easy to crowd out: the wish to finish something difficult, learn about an unfamiliar place, stay with a person through an awkward pause, or spend an evening without producing anything visible.

Some interests become clear only after we have given them time. A system that continually supplies what we already appear to like may narrow the occasions on which a new interest can emerge. The result need not be a dramatic manipulation. It can be a gradual reduction in the variety of experience from which a life develops.

The unprofitable moment

There are moments whose value cannot be inferred from continued engagement with a service. A map succeeds when a person arrives and stops consulting it. A good explanation may allow someone to close the interface and try the task. A useful reminder disappears into an action performed elsewhere.

The successful outcome can therefore look like departure. This creates a tension wherever a service is rewarded mainly for keeping us present inside it. A product can be delightful and still need a better answer to the question of when it should let us go.

Design can acknowledge an ending. A system might provide the requested material without turning every completion into a new obligation. It might make a boundary easy to set and equally easy to understand. Such choices are not acts of charity toward weak users. They recognize that people have purposes beyond the product.

Institutions have parallel responsibilities. A workplace cannot tell employees to protect attention while celebrating instant replies at every hour. A school cannot criticize children's distraction while requiring a confusing collection of notifications for ordinary participation. The environment communicates the real expectation more forcefully than the poster on the wall.

The person repairing the chair eventually returns to it. A joint has loosened. The repair is less elegant than the video suggested. There is glue on the floor and a screw left over that seems important. A family member sits down too early and is told to stand up immediately.

The room has not become a photograph worth sharing. The chair may hold. Something needed doing, and somebody did it. There are forms of satisfaction that become available only when attention returns from the possible life to the life in front of us.

CHAPTER 05

A World Without Waiting

On a cold morning in an airport, the departures board went red. A storm had settled over the region, canceling flights faster than the airline could assign new ones. The terminal filled with stranded people performing the modern ritual of disrupted plans: refreshing apps, joining digital queues, opening laptops, negotiating by text, photographing the board as if the camera might produce a different answer.

Near the gate, a boy of perhaps seven asked his father what they were supposed to do. The father studied his phone and said, "Wait." The child accepted this for eleven seconds. Then he asked what he could do while he waited. His father passed him a tablet without looking up. The boy disappeared into it, the storm disappeared, and the waiting was over even though neither of them had moved.

This was an act of kindness. Anyone who has traveled with a restless child understands it. The father was tired, the gate was loud, and the tablet bought peace in a situation neither could control. Civilization is built partly from such mercies. The point is not to turn a weary parent into a symbol of decline. The point is to notice how thoroughly we have come to regard waiting as a defect that technology ought to repair.

Waiting once occupied more of daily life because travel, communication, and household work took longer. Much of that time was tedious, exhausting, or dangerous. Faster transport, refrigeration, and reliable services removed real burdens. No one needs a delay at the pharmacy to develop character.

Yet waiting did more than waste time. It placed us inside time. It reminded us that the world did not answer instantly to desire. A letter required faith in an unseen journey. A photograph had to be developed before it could be judged. A question might remain open until a knowledgeable person or a library became available. In those intervals, anticipation accumulated. Imagination went to work. The self encountered its own company.

We can become accustomed to a speed that is impossible for people to maintain. An unanswered message starts to feel like a statement about the relationship. A slow reply becomes something to explain. Before treating either as an insult, it is worth remembering that we rarely know what else is happening at the other end.

Convenience removes burdens, and many deserve removing. It can also change what we practice. Navigation saves us from being lost; relying on it every time may leave us less familiar with a place. Automated checkout can shorten a queue and remove a small exchange with another person. Whether the trade is worthwhile depends on the life in which it occurs. A tired caregiver and a lonely retiree may need different things from the same service.

There is an old temptation to romanticize hardship from a safe distance. Suffering does not automatically ennoble anyone. Poverty, disease, discrimination, and violence can crush human possibility; removing them is not a spiritual loss. We should not preserve pain to manufacture character. The meaningful distinction is between suffering that diminishes life and difficulty that develops it, between pointless barriers and formative resistance. The fact that the line is difficult to draw does not absolve us from drawing it.

Consider a child learning to tie a shoe. An adult can end the struggle in seconds. On a morning when the bus is coming, that may be the kindest choice. On another morning, waiting allows frustration to become concentration and concentration to become coordination. The knot matters less than the discovery that a difficult task can become possible. Helping well requires noticing which morning this is.

AI can end some kinds of waiting usefully: locating information to verify, translating a sentence, or organizing information we would otherwise search for. Other questions need time because our own response is still forming. A quick answer can be available before we know whether it answers what was troubling us.

An unresolved question is not always an emergency. You may need to think about a difficult conversation, spend time with an unfamiliar idea, or let your reaction to news settle before deciding what it means. AI can offer perspectives during that process. Its readiness to answer does not require you to be ready to conclude.

The route and the place

Consider an imagined visit to an unfamiliar town. A navigation tool guides a traveler from the station to a friend's apartment. This is a genuine convenience, especially if the traveler is carrying luggage, navigating with a disability, or arriving after dark. Arriving safely matters more than performing independence for its own sake.

The next morning, with different circumstances and no urgent deadline, the traveler walks the same route. Now there is time to notice a bakery, the sound of a schoolyard, a bench under a tree. The town begins to acquire a shape beyond the sequence of turns. Something has been gained that the original tool was not necessarily designed to provide.

The conclusion is not that navigation should be abandoned. It is that a route and a place are different kinds of knowledge. A person may need both. Technology can help with the first while leaving space for the second, provided that arriving efficiently does not become the sole purpose of every movement.

This is true beyond geography. A summary can provide an overview without providing the experience of reading an argument unfold. A suggested reply can help a person begin without revealing what they will discover by listening. A generated plan can organize an activity without supplying the meaning of undertaking it.

We need not choose one form of knowledge forever. We can ask what the situation calls for. There are days when the summary is exactly what we need, and days when it keeps us from encountering the part we would not have known to request.

Permission to be unfinished

Many parts of life cannot be hurried into completeness. A friendship needs repeated encounters. Grief changes shape unevenly. Trust may take longer to restore than the apology took to compose. A child can understand the words of an explanation before being ready to live by them.

These are not failures of optimization. They are features of lives whose meaning depends on time, bodies, memory, and relationships. Faster information can help us within them. It does not necessarily accelerate the whole process.

An environment full of instant production may make unfinishedness feel embarrassing. We can generate a polished plan in seconds, so why are we still uncertain about the decision? We can receive an elegant account of healthy communication, so why did the conversation with our sibling go badly? The comparison mistakes the availability of a description for the acquisition of a capacity.

Some patience is simply permission to continue learning without pretending that knowing the language has completed the work. This kind of patience is compatible with urgency about injustice, suffering, and preventable obstacles. We can move quickly to provide help while accepting that a person is not a project to be completed on schedule.

At the airport, the power outlets filled before the seats did. People arranged themselves along walls, tethered to chargers. An elderly woman unfolded a paper crossword. Two strangers began talking after one asked whether the other's phone had service. The boy's tablet eventually lost its charge. He complained, negotiated, and then, receiving no alternative, pressed his forehead to the glass.

Snow moved sideways beyond the runway lights. A baggage cart crept across the white distance. The boy watched it vanish and return. He drew a shape in the fog his breath left on the window, erased it with his sleeve, and drew another. After a while he pointed outside and said something to his father. This time the father put down his phone.

His father followed the shape on the glass, then pointed toward another cart moving slowly through the snow. For a few minutes neither looked back at the gate.

CHAPTER 06

Keep Learning When Answers Are Easy

Eli asked an AI assistant to explain a homework problem. The explanation was patient and clear. He followed each line while it was on the screen. The next afternoon, faced with a slightly different question in class, he could not decide how to begin.

It was tempting to blame the tool. It was also tempting to ask it for the next answer. Neither would tell him which part he had actually learned. After school, he returned to the explanation, covered the worked steps, and tried again. He got stuck earlier than he expected.

This time he asked for a hint at that step. He made another attempt, then asked for a similar problem without its solution. It took longer. At the end, he could explain why he had chosen the first move. The useful result was something he could do after closing the conversation.

Questions about learning also matter at work. The International Labour Organization's 2023 analysis describes occupations as bundles of tasks, with different exposure to automation and assistance. If a tool changes some tasks, people may need new ways to develop the judgment the whole job requires. [7]

Experienced people can use assistance differently. A translator may know enough to judge a proposed phrase; a beginner may not hear what is wrong with it. The same output can therefore be helpful to one person and misleading to another. Confidence in the tool should not exceed our ability to check the work, especially when someone else will rely on it.

In a 2023 experiment published in Science, Shakked Noy and Whitney Zhang found that access to generative AI improved speed and average quality on professional writing tasks. That result is evidence about the tasks and participants studied, not a promise about every kind of work. [8]

Michelle Vaccaro, Abdullah Almaatouq, and Thomas Malone's 2024 meta-analysis of 106 experimental studies found that human-AI combinations, on average, outperformed humans alone but performed worse than the better of humans or AI alone. Results varied with the task and the relative performance of the participants. Adding a person to a system does not, by itself, make the system stronger. The relationship has to be designed and tested. [9]

You do not need to turn every assisted task into a lesson. Some work is simply work you need finished. Be honest about which outcome you want: a completed task, practice at a skill, or both. Choose help accordingly. A polished result can satisfy the first goal while concealing that the second has not happened.

Two different promises

The phrase AI in education can conceal several different promises. It may mean that students can produce more correct work. It may mean that they understand more, remember more, or become more able to solve a new problem. It may mean that teachers have more time to teach. These outcomes are related, but they are not interchangeable.

The difference matters because a finished assignment is visible. Learning is harder to see. A student can hand in an excellent response and remain unable to explain how it works. Another can produce an imperfect response that reveals substantial progress. A system judged only by the completed product may reward the wrong kind of success.

Two research examples help clarify the distinction. In a six-week program in Nigeria, secondary-school students received teacher-supported generative-AI tutoring focused on English, AI knowledge, and digital skills. A randomized evaluation found improved measured learning, with an overall effect of roughly 0.3 standard deviations. This was a specific, supported program, not a finding that unrestricted chatbot access universally improves education. [10]

In a separate experiment involving nearly a thousand mathematics students at one high school in Turkey, a chatbot that could supply answers improved assisted practice but was followed by worse performance on an unassisted exam than the control condition. The reported reduction was 17 percent. A tutor designed with learning safeguards largely removed that negative effect; it did not establish a positive exam advantage. The design and setting limit how widely the results can be generalized. [11]

These studies should not be collapsed into a slogan that AI either teaches or prevents learning. Their value is in making us ask what kind of assistance, for what purpose, under which conditions. A good answer to those questions will involve teachers and students, not only software capabilities.

The help that leaves something behind

Imagine two learners encountering the same difficult paragraph. One asks for a simpler version, reads it, and moves on. The other uses the simpler version to return to the original, noticing which phrases now make sense and where a question remains. The same initial assistance has entered two different learning processes.

There is no need to shame the first learner. Perhaps they only needed the information for a practical decision. Perhaps the task was never intended to develop reading skill. But if the goal was learning, the second process leaves more opportunity for the learner to participate. The purpose determines what counts as adequate help.

The person providing help must calibrate it. Too little support can leave a student excluded and discouraged. Too much can turn the student into an observer of someone else's competence. Good teaching is partly the difficult art of finding the next achievable stretch. A technology designed for learning should be judged by how it supports that process, not merely by how quickly it displays a correct result.

This principle applies to adults as well. A worker adopting a new system may need explanations, practice, and permission to ask elementary questions. An older person learning to use a service may need the steps connected to a purpose they recognize. Nobody becomes less worthy because a change has made them a beginner again.

The quiet child who asks again

In an illustrative classroom scene, a student does not raise her hand. She has missed one step in a lesson, and every later step has become a new reason to stay silent. By the time the teacher asks whether anyone has questions, she no longer knows where to begin.

Later, an accessible tutoring tool allows her to ask the same basic question several times. She can request a different explanation without feeling that a room is waiting for her. On this occasion, the privacy helps her attempt what embarrassment prevented. The value is not that the tool is infinitely patient in a human sense. It is that the student has gained an opportunity to participate.

The teacher still matters. The system may misunderstand a question or give a convincing but wrong explanation. It may miss an earlier gap in learning, a language barrier, or a problem outside school. Someone must still be able to see where the learner is stuck and help them move beyond it.

The imagined student eventually brings a question to class. It is more specific now. She can name the step that still troubles her. The tool has not replaced her teacher; it has helped her reach the teacher with a question she can bear to ask.

That is a powerful kind of progress. It should be available to students who cannot buy private support as well as to those who can. It also depends on matters that enthusiasm alone cannot supply: access, appropriate content, privacy, supervision, and a way to evaluate whether the student is actually learning.

Knowledge that belongs to us

Why learn something a machine can explain? The question sounds practical until we examine what knowledge makes possible. Understanding allows us to recognize when an explanation is incomplete, connect a new idea to an old one, ask a more precise question, and notice a consequence the original task did not include.

Knowledge is also part of participation in a shared world. Knowing enough about history to question a convenient story, enough about numbers to recognize a misleading comparison, or enough about biology to ask an informed question can change how freely a person moves through decisions made around them.

This does not mean every individual must become an expert in everything. Human societies depend on divided knowledge and justified trust. The challenge is to preserve enough understanding to know where trust belongs, what would challenge it, and when another kind of help is needed.

AI can enlarge access to explanations. That is a significant opportunity. But if access becomes an excuse to stop developing understanding, we may acquire an abundance of answers while becoming less able to evaluate the people and systems supplying them. A person who can always obtain a response is not necessarily a person who can judge a response.

There is pleasure here too. Learning is not only preparation for employment or defense against deception. It can alter the texture of an ordinary day. A bird becomes a recognizable species. A building reveals the decisions of people who lived before us. A song acquires a history. The world becomes more interesting because we have become more able to meet it.

A fair account of effort

Effort is often discussed as though everybody begins with the same resources. They do not. A student caring for siblings after school, a learner with an inaccessible textbook, and a classmate with a quiet room and private tutor do not face the same assignment in the same circumstances. Technology can help reduce some differences. It can also create new ones.

The appropriate question is not whether assistance makes a task easier. Education is full of assistance. The question is whether the help makes learning more possible while preserving meaningful participation. A reader using text-to-speech is still reading in a significant educational sense. A student receiving a translation may finally be able to engage the concept instead of being blocked by language.

Distinguishing accommodation from replacement requires attention to the purpose of the task and the needs of the learner. Blanket suspicion can be as damaging as uncritical adoption. A child should not have to defend every use of support as though independence were the only respectable way to learn.

The future classroom will need more than a rule about whether a tool is allowed. It will need a clear account of what students are learning, how they can show that learning, and where assistance fits. Oral explanation, revision, practice, discussion, and work over time may reveal things a polished final submission cannot.

Those are educational choices, not a demand that every teacher suddenly do unlimited additional work. Schools need to provide the time, training, and support that thoughtful changes require. Asking teachers to solve a technological transition through unpaid vigilance is not a humane strategy.

The best assistance should make the learner more present in the learning. That is a different ambition from making the learner's output appear effortlessly complete.

CHAPTER 07

Raising the Unfinished

The children had been promised nothing. No entertainer was coming. No screen would be passed around. The adults were talking beneath the trees, and the afternoon had opened into that familiar, unbearable territory: there was nothing to do.

For several minutes they performed their misery publicly. One kicked the leg of a picnic table. Another asked how much longer they had to stay. A third lay dramatically in the grass as if boredom were a weather event from which rescue should already have arrived. Their complaints received sympathy but no solution.

Then a stick became a boundary. The space beyond it became dangerous. Pinecones acquired value. Two children began building a shelter that could not shelter anyone. An argument arose about the rules of a game nobody had known existed ten minutes earlier. By late afternoon, the adults had to call them repeatedly before they came.

Boredom has been tried and convicted in the court of modern life. We describe it as vacancy, failure, the absence of something better. Products promise to eliminate it from travel, exercise, meals, waiting rooms, bedrooms, and the seconds before sleep. The promise sounds humane because boredom can be painful. Prolonged, imposed monotony can diminish people. A worker trapped in repetitive labor or an elderly person isolated without meaningful contact does not need a lecture about creativity.

But not every unstimulated moment is deprivation. Some are thresholds. When the external world stops supplying novelty, the mind begins generating its own material. Memories combine. Problems loosen. Images arrive without being summoned. The wandering mind does not always produce genius; frequently it produces nonsense. Creativity depends partly on our willingness to tolerate that waste.

Studies of idle thought offer a limited but useful finding. Quentin Raffaelli and colleagues found associations between creativity and more exploratory thought during rest. A 2025 writing experiment by Colin McDaniel and colleagues linked more mind wandering during a break with improvement on computational measures when participants returned to the same story prompt; human judges' creativity ratings did not show the same relationship. The different break activities did not produce significant differences in improvement. Neither study establishes that boredom causes creativity. They leave room to take unfilled time seriously without making it a cure. [12]

Many discoveries carry a period of apparent uselessness inside them. A scientist walks away from the bench. A composer hears a phrase while doing dishes. A writer realizes the ending while driving a familiar road. Insight can seem sudden even when it follows a long period of thought.

The attention economy has difficulty valuing incubation. A blank interval cannot display an advertisement unless it is filled. A workplace cannot measure the idea that has not yet formed. A school anxious about achievement may schedule every hour, then wonder why children wait to be instructed. We create lives dense with inputs and call the resulting exhaustion a shortage of creativity.

Artificial intelligence can generate options when we are stuck. It can also fill the pause before we have worked out what we want. Choosing from useful suggestions may be part of creativity. It becomes a problem when we never discover what we would have tried without them.

The discipline of boredom is not heroic deprivation. It is leaving certain spaces uncolonized. Walking without audio. Waiting without reaching. Letting a child complain long enough to discover what comes after complaint. Sitting with a problem after the obvious answers have been exhausted.

Stories, games, and music are among humanity's richest creations. The question is whether we choose them or reach for them whenever a moment feels unfilled. Children need opportunities to invent their own play as well as opportunities to enjoy what other people have made.

At the picnic, the shelter collapsed before anyone left. The builders regarded the disaster for one solemn second, then decided the ruins were a ship. The same sticks entered another world.

Distraction in the classroom

In PISA 2022, about thirty percent of students across OECD countries reported distraction from their own digital-device use in most or every mathematics lesson; about a quarter reported distraction from other students' devices. Frequent distraction was associated with lower mathematics performance after adjustment for socioeconomic differences. This is survey evidence, not proof that a device caused a particular student's score.

The findings were mixed. Moderate use of devices for learning was associated with stronger performance in some comparisons. A screen can support a lesson while also carrying messages, games, and distractions. Schools need to examine the purpose, setting, and use rather than treat the device as one uniform intervention. [13]

Childhood is not an inefficient version of adulthood

A little girl sat in the back seat and asked where the moon went during the day. Her father began answering, then stopped. He knew he could summon a perfect animation, an expert explanation, and photographs from space before the next traffic light. Instead he asked what she thought.

She considered the question seriously. Perhaps the moon became transparent. Perhaps it followed another family. Perhaps daylight was so loud that nobody could hear it. The answers were wrong and magnificent. They revealed a mind constructing the universe before receiving it fully assembled.

Childhood is not an inefficient version of adulthood. It is a protected period of incompleteness. Children misread, invent, imitate, fail, depend, and slowly learn to govern attention, emotion, appetite, and relationship. A society reveals what it believes about human development through the pressures it allows to reach them.

Digital technology has opened extraordinary doors for children. It can make language visible to a deaf student, connect an isolated learner to instruction, offer adaptive practice, and give a curious child access to museums, music, maps, and explanations once unavailable. UNESCO's global education work documents both this potential and the unequal access that still divides it.

The same evidence counsels humility. UNESCO's 2023 Global Education Monitoring Report emphasized that robust evidence for educational technology is often scarce, products change faster than evaluation, devices can distract from learning, and children's data may be exposed. The report's title asked the right question: technology in education - a tool on whose terms? [14]

The American Psychological Association's health advisory on adolescent social media use rejected simple claims that social media is inherently good or bad. Effects vary with a young person's development, vulnerability, content, context, and patterns of use. That complexity is not permission to do nothing. It means adults cannot outsource judgment to slogans or age limits alone. [15]

Children are asked to manage social comparison while identity is forming, permanent records while judgment is developing, and personalized persuasion before they fully understand the business model. Useful access requires accompaniment and limits that change as a child becomes more capable.

Parents face an unfair contest. The device is portable, socially necessary, educational, entertaining, and designed by institutions with more behavioral knowledge than most families possess. Adults are also exhausted and implicated. We cannot credibly demand that children put screens away while giving them the remainder of our attention.

Generative AI adds a new choice for a child who is stuck: help can arrive before an adult notices the difficulty. That can be welcome. The child still needs guidance about what to ask, what to check, what information to keep private, and which parts of an assignment they are expected to do themselves.

UNESCO's 2023 guidance on generative AI in education places human agency, privacy, inclusion, and educational purpose at the center of these decisions. Those principles concern the conditions adults create around a child's use, not merely the appearance of a finished assignment. [16]

A child needs adults who sometimes know more and sometimes say, honestly, "I don't know." The sentence protects wonder. It demonstrates that ignorance is not humiliation but an invitation. If every question is closed instantly, curiosity can become consumption rather than a way of inhabiting the world.

Some parts of childhood need protection from continuous evaluation: play that is not recorded, a disagreement repaired without an audience, a first attempt that can be awkward. Children also need adults who can distinguish a struggle worth attempting from one that requires support. The boundary will differ with age, disability, temperament, and the task.

The father in the car eventually explained why the moon can remain in the daytime sky. His daughter listened, corrected parts of her imaginary theory, and asked a harder question. Knowledge did not destroy wonder. It gave wonder a larger world.

The girl looked again through the window. The moon was faint in the blue afternoon, present all along.

They are already in the future

Adults can discuss the future as though children will arrive in it only when they begin work. Children already inhabit the environments we are building. They form expectations about answers, authority, attention, and friendship while those environments are still being debated.

Preparation therefore means more than teaching a child how to operate a tool. It includes helping them recognize the difference between a suggestion and a command, a confident response and a justified claim, an entertaining simulation and a relationship with another person. These distinctions develop through repeated experiences and conversations, not a single warning.

An adult who says never trust AI and then uses it carelessly teaches a confusing lesson. So does an adult who describes every difficulty as something technology should immediately remove. Children watch what we rely on, what we check, and what we are willing to admit we do not know.

In a fictional kitchen conversation, Sofia asks whether a generated picture shows a real animal. Daniel answers too quickly that it does. Eli looks more closely and notices that the feet do not make sense. Daniel could defend his first response or turn the moment into a lecture about the dangers of technology. Instead, he admits that he assumed the picture was real because it looked convincing.

Sofia asks how they can tell. They look for the original source. The answer is not all she learns. She sees an adult make a mistake, someone question it, and the family investigate without treating the question as disobedience.

A person rather than a prediction

Personalized education can promise to meet a child where they are. That is an appealing aim. But a child is also someone whose interests, capacities, and circumstances may change. A description of their current performance should not quietly become a limit on what adults expect of them.

Imagine a system that repeatedly offers a student easier material because earlier answers were weak. There may be good reasons to rebuild foundations. There may also be a risk that the student rarely encounters the challenge through which a new interest could emerge. The question is whether the arrangement remains open to change, surprise, and informed human judgment.

The same concern applies to behavioral labels. An adult's shorthand can already follow a child from one classroom to another. A stored profile may make that shorthand more durable. A humane educational system needs ways for people to outgrow the descriptions used to support them.

This is not an argument against remembering a student's needs. Forgetting can force a family to fight the same battle repeatedly. The issue is who controls the record, how it can be corrected, and whether it makes room for the developing person rather than treating the person as a completed interpretation.

Children deserve protection and participation. A young child cannot evaluate every data practice, so adults carry responsibilities the child cannot carry alone. As children mature, they also need age-appropriate explanations and a voice in decisions that affect them. Protection should help agency develop, not make it permanently unnecessary.

The right to ordinary experience

Not every childhood activity needs to be optimized for future achievement. A game can be worth playing because it is fun. A drawing can matter because a child wanted to make it. An afternoon can contain aimlessness without becoming wasted potential.

AI may help children explore interests and access material that would otherwise be unavailable. That can be wonderful. It should not make every curiosity the beginning of a personalized improvement program. A child is allowed to abandon a project, return to it later, or enjoy it without becoming exceptional.

The pressure to produce can enter through loving intentions. Adults want to prepare children, protect them, and avoid missing an opportunity. Yet a childhood organized entirely around what the child might become can leave too little room for the person they already are.

Sofia's questions sometimes need an answer. Sometimes they need a companion willing to look with her. An explanation of the moon can deepen wonder; an adult stepping outside to notice it with her can give that wonder a relationship. There is no reason to make those experiences enemies.

The future we owe children should contain capable tools and adults who remain willing to be there. It should leave them informed enough to use technology and free enough to develop purposes that technology did not choose for them.

The Cost Comes Home

Route 17

Daniel's distribution center measured nearly everything. It measured units picked per hour, time between scans, accuracy, idle minutes, overtime, damaged inventory, and the distance each worker walked. A monitor above the floor displayed the shift's progress in green, yellow, or red.

Daniel understood why. Eleven thousand orders moved through the building on an ordinary day. A missing part could stop a repair shop two states away. Measurement found waste, and waste became cost, and cost eventually became someone's job.

Still, there were things the screen could not see.

It could not see that Calvin on Route 17 had begun moving slowly because his wife was receiving chemotherapy and neither of them had slept. It recorded only that his rate had fallen nine percent. It could not see that Priya kept correcting inventory errors left by a new employee because she remembered what it felt like to be new. The system credited the correction but not the kindness. It could not see that Daniel sometimes spent seven minutes listening to an employee who needed four, because the first three minutes were usually the story people believed they were allowed to tell.

One Thursday, headquarters sent a ranking of supervisors. Daniel was in the middle. His director advised him to reduce untracked conversations.

"They add up," the director said.

"Calvin needs help right now," Daniel said.

He started explaining about Calvin's wife, then lost his place. The director was waiting. Daniel knew his team's numbers were down and that the conversation would not improve them. He asked for time anyway.

The following month, Calvin's wife died. He missed four shifts, then returned because bereavement leave had run out. Daniel met him at the entrance and walked beside him across the enormous floor. Nothing in the management system instructed him to do this. Nothing prohibited it either.

At Station 42, Calvin stopped.

"I don't know how people come back," he said.

Daniel looked at the rows of conveyor belts and blinking scanners. He had no answer that could survive contact with the question.

"You don't have to know today," he said. "Just stay near me."

For the rest of the morning, Daniel's numbers were poor. Priya covered part of his route and stayed late to finish her own work. He thanked her, then realized that thanks would not give her the evening back.

At the next staffing review, he asked for temporary coverage. He did not receive everything he requested. Calvin still needed support, and the work still had to move. Care had entered the schedule; it had not made the arithmetic disappear.

Interpretation

The patient spoke a Mixtec language. The hospital's video interpretation service offered Spanish, which was her second language and not one she trusted when frightened. Her daughter tried to help, but she was twelve, and the conversation concerned surgery.

Maya watched the child's face tighten as the physician described probabilities. No child should have to choose the words that might persuade a mother to consent.

The hospital had recently introduced an AI translation tool. On simple, nonclinical exchanges it could be useful: asking about a meal preference or explaining where a visitor should wait. A surgical discussion demanded more than a plausible sentence on a screen.

This was not routine.

Maya requested a qualified interpreter who spoke the patient's language variety. The estimated wait was forty-five minutes. The operating schedule was already slipping. A coordinator asked whether the daughter and translation tool could cover the essentials.

"The essentials are whether she understands what may happen to her body," Maya said.

The physician confirmed that this discussion could wait. Maya explained the delay to the patient and her daughter. They waited.

The interpreter joined from another state. She did more than replace words. She noticed when the patient's silence meant uncertainty rather than agreement. She asked the physician to describe risk without idiom. She clarified a family term whose literal translation suggested a different relationship. The patient asked eight questions. Through her daughter, she had asked none.

Afterward, the girl went to the vending machine. Maya found her staring at the rows.

"You did a good job," Maya said.

The girl shook her head. "I didn't know how to say the bad parts."

"You weren't supposed to."

She began to cry with the relief of someone released from a responsibility adults had mistaken for competence.

The list

The list contained eleven names. Daniel had been told to reduce the afternoon shift by eight.

Management called it a capacity adjustment. The phrase arrived in a slide deck beside a graph showing the growing accuracy of automated picking systems. Demand had softened. Equipment had improved. The building could move the same volume with fewer people.

Daniel knew the arithmetic. He also knew the names.

One belonged to a man supporting two households. One belonged to a woman six weeks from vesting in the retirement plan. One belonged to an employee who had been warned twice and probably expected the call. One belonged to Priya, who solved problems the tracking system did not record because she prevented them before they became tickets.

The director advised supervisors not to personalize the process.

"I need to check how these names were chosen," Daniel said.

He spent the night at the kitchen table after everyone slept. He reviewed attendance, performance, certifications, disciplinary notes, cross-training, and the assumptions inside the staffing model. At one in the morning, Rosa found him surrounded by paper.

"Can you save them?" she asked.

"Not all."

Rosa poured water and sat down. She had cleaned hotel rooms after arriving in Texas. Once, a manager dismissed six housekeepers at the end of a shift and collected their uniforms before they could leave.

"Then do not make them feel thrown away," she said.

The next day Daniel challenged two names where the model had mistaken lower scan counts for lower value. He secured four weeks of transitional scheduling for three others and insisted that every affected employee receive the news from a person who knew their work.

Eight jobs still disappeared. One of the affected workers asked Daniel why there had been money for equipment but not for another month of wages. Daniel explained the decision as plainly as he could. The explanation did not make the worker less angry. He stayed through the conversation without asking to be forgiven.

PART 3

The Lives Between Us

A relationship is more than a response.

CHAPTER 08

The Distance Between Us

The restaurant was almost empty by the time the old man reached across the table and touched the woman's hand. Rain had begun after dinner, not hard enough to drive anyone indoors but enough to turn the pavement black and glossy. Streetlights trembled in the windows. A bartender polished glasses with the patient resignation of someone waiting for the last tables to leave, and from the kitchen came the bright metallic crash of a pan being dropped, followed by laughter.

The couple near the window had finished eating. Their plates were gone; their wine remained. The man leaned forward as he spoke, and the woman listened with an attention so complete it seemed almost physical. Both of her hands rested around one of his. Perhaps he was telling her something important. Perhaps he was telling a story she had heard for forty years. There was no way to know, and it did not matter. She watched him as if the story deserved a home.

Across the room, a younger couple sat looking at separate phones. A delivery driver refreshed an order screen. A tablet chimed behind the counter. It was impossible to know what any of them was doing: working, avoiding a conversation, or checking on someone they loved. The older couple's attention was easier to see.

The man said something that made the woman laugh. Not the careful laugh offered to be kind, but the helpless kind that briefly takes possession of the body. She leaned back, eyes closed, then shook her head at him with the practiced affection of someone who had accepted his ridiculousness long ago. When the laughter ended, silence entered the space between them. Neither reached for a device. Neither tried to fill it. They simply remained.

The width of a table

Human beings have always found ways to leave the room without moving. We have stared through windows, wandered inside memories, read newspapers at breakfast, and hidden behind work. Nostalgia lies when it tells us previous generations offered one another undivided attention. They did not. But our exits were once slower and less abundant. Today a pause of three seconds can open into an infinite corridor: headlines, messages, photographs, arguments, games, purchases, videos, work, strangers, outrage. The smallest emptiness now has a door, and we have trained our hands to open it before we realize we are leaving.

The word connection has become slippery. Engineers use it to describe the successful exchange of signals. Platforms use it to describe the addition of another name to a network. People use it to describe the feeling of being seen. These meanings overlap, but they are not the same. A device can be connected while its owner is alone. A person can be surrounded and still be unseen. The network can grow while the relationship weakens.

Long-distance communication was once an event. A letter crossed mountains in a bag. A transatlantic cable compressed weeks into minutes. The telephone carried a human voice into rooms where the body could not go. Each invention reduced distance, and rightly astonished the people who received it. A mother could hear from a son in another city. A doctor could be summoned. A family could learn that someone had arrived safely. We did not build communication technology because we wanted less of one another. We built it because absence hurt.

The smartphone keeps the distant close, offers maps to the lost, and places emergency help within reach. It allows grandparents to watch children grow across oceans. That is part of its value. At the table, however, the same device makes every distant person and unfinished task available to compete with the person already there.

An interruption once had to announce itself: a knock at the door, a telephone ringing on the wall. Now it can rest quietly beside the plate. Even before a screen lights up, we know what might arrive through it. The person opposite us knows too.

A glance at a screen can land badly when someone is trying to tell us something. It can also be necessary. Saying what we are doing helps: "I need to check that she got home. Then I want to hear the rest." The explanation only earns trust if we actually return.

We can return a call or ask someone to start again. We cannot always recover the moment in which they were ready to speak. That does not make every interruption unforgivable. It gives us a reason to notice which interruptions have become a pattern.

The old couple at the restaurant eventually asked for the check. The man helped the woman into her coat with a care that suggested repetition rather than performance. Outside, he opened an umbrella and tilted it toward her, leaving his own shoulder in the rain. They moved slowly across the shining sidewalk, close enough to share the small circle of shelter.

From across the restaurant, it was impossible to know whether they were happy. A single beautiful moment proves little about a marriage. Perhaps they would argue in the car. For the length of one dinner, however, they kept choosing the place where they were.

One in six

In its 2025 report, the World Health Organization's Commission on Social Connection estimated that roughly one person in six worldwide experienced loneliness. Reported rates were particularly high among adolescents and young adults and in low-income countries. The estimate gives scale to an experience that people often conceal. [17]

Loneliness and isolation are not interchangeable. A person may enjoy living alone and still have dependable relationships; another may feel lonely in a busy household. The useful question is whether the connection available matches the connection the person wants.

In a 2010 meta-analysis, Julianne Holt-Lunstad, Timothy B. Smith, and J. Bradley Layton combined 148 studies involving more than 300,000 participants. Stronger social relationships were associated with a greater likelihood of survival. That association does not prove that prescribing company will lengthen a particular person's life. It does give reason to take relationships seriously in discussions of health. [18]

Contact is not connection

At 2:17 in the morning, a man sat on the edge of his bed and scrolled through 1,842 contacts. The number was absurd. It represented colleagues from several jobs, former classmates, vendors, neighbors, relatives, parents from school, people met once at conferences, and names he no longer recognized. He was, by the ordinary measures of the connected age, surrounded.

His marriage had ended that evening. The argument was not dramatic enough for a film. There had been no broken glass, no final revelation, only the exhausted admission that two people who once knew each other intimately had spent years becoming efficient partners in a household and strangers everywhere else. After his wife left to stay with her sister, the silence in the house became unbearable. He wanted to hear another human voice.

He moved through the names slowly. Some belonged to people he liked but did not trust with grief. Some were too entangled with work. Some would answer but require a performance: the funny version, the competent version, the version that already knew how the story ended. Several people had once been close, but friendship had been maintained through likes and holiday texts until the appearance of relationship outlived the relationship itself.

He finally called a college friend he had not spoken with in nearly a year. The friend answered on the fourth ring and said only, "What happened?" There was no irritation in his voice, no demand for an apology about the hour. The man tried to speak and discovered that language had been holding the door shut. When it opened, he wept.

A crowded city can intensify loneliness. A marriage can conceal it. A person can carry it through an office where everyone knows his title and nobody knows his fear.

Our age offers extraordinary tools against isolation. A rare-disease patient can find another person who understands. A teenager in a hostile community can discover that she is not alone. Families scattered by work and migration can gather on a screen. People with disabilities or limited mobility can enter communities previously closed by geography. These are not lesser relationships simply because technology helps carry them.

The problem begins when connection becomes confused with contact. Contact is easy to accumulate. It asks little, scales beautifully, and leaves numbers behind. Relationship is stubbornly inefficient. It requires repetition, patience, repair, and the willingness to be altered by another person's needs. A network expands by addition. A friendship deepens by attention.

The architecture of many platforms encourages us to present rather than reveal. Presentation is not dishonesty; every social setting contains performance. But a life lived continually before an audience can make vulnerability feel like bad branding. We polish the kitchen before the photograph, announce the promotion before admitting the panic, and post from the vacation while arguing off camera. Everyone understands that the image is partial, yet repeated exposure to other people's partial lives can make our whole life feel inadequate.

Intimacy can begin with something small enough to risk: "It has been a hard week." The response helps us decide whether to say more. Trust grows partly through those decisions. We do not owe our most private story to someone just because they ask for it.

The man on the bed spoke with his old friend until nearly dawn. His friend did not solve the marriage. He offered no perfect sentence. Once, he misunderstood and had to ask again. A dog barked in the background. There were long silences and the sound of a coffee maker starting in another house hundreds of miles away. The conversation was clumsy, repetitive, and alive.

Before they hung up, the friend said, "You should have called sooner." It was not an accusation. It was an opening.

The following afternoon, the man looked again at the long list of names. The number had not changed, but its meaning had. He began calling people, not to announce the crisis to everyone but to stop pretending friendship could survive indefinitely on evidence of continued existence. Some conversations were awkward. One went unanswered. Another friend said, with painful honesty, that he had also wondered where the years had gone.

For someone without an old friend to call, this story may sound like advice from a life they do not have. "Reach out" is much easier to say when there is already someone to reach.

A beginning can be less demanding than a late-night confession. Return to a place where the same people meet. Ask an acquaintance to have coffee after the activity you already share. Send a specific invitation rather than "We should catch up." A familiar face may become a dependable person over time; it does not have to become one immediately.

Some invitations will go unanswered. That can hurt without proving anything final about your worth. Try a different person or a different setting. The friend who cannot talk tonight may be able to talk tomorrow. A relationship needs room for both people's limits as well as their need for company.

Across a kitchen and an ocean

Consider another illustrative household, far from the restaurant. A grandmother has placed a tablet against a jar so that it faces the kitchen table. Her grandson lives in another country. Their call has been delayed twice because his mother works evenings and the connection has been unreliable.

When he appears, he wants to show her a tooth that has fallen out. He moves too close to the camera. She sees an enormous eye, then the ceiling, then the gap in his mouth. They laugh. She asks him a question in the language she grew up speaking. He answers partly in that language and partly in the one he uses at school.

His mother helps with a word. A translation feature helps with another. The conversation is uneven. The boy becomes distracted by something outside the frame. His grandmother waits while he retrieves a picture. For a few minutes, the distance is not gone, but it has become less absolute.

Calling this encounter less real because a screen carries it would miss the people inside it. Their affection is not virtual in the sense of being imaginary. The medium has limitations, but the relationship does not begin and end with those limitations. It contains history, obligation, delight, and the ordinary difficulty of finding time.

Technology can be a way of leaving the room. It can also be the only available way into a room. Any account of human connection that forgets the second fact will be least useful to many of the people who need connection most.

What continuity requires

There is a difference between an impressive moment of contact and a relationship that can be relied upon. The grandmother's call matters partly because another call is expected. A child can bring an unfinished story to the next conversation. The people involved remember enough to ask how it turned out.

Continuity does not require uninterrupted availability. People have jobs, illness, competing commitments, and different capacities for communication. A relationship can be dependable even when contact is infrequent. What matters is whether expectations are sufficiently understood and whether absence can be discussed without constant guessing.

A scheduled call is not yet a kept promise. The relationship grows when someone returns.

There is also a difference between remembering a fact and remembering a person. A system may retrieve the name of someone's school or the date of a difficult anniversary. That can be useful. Human remembering includes an understanding that the fact belongs to a life that may have changed. The anniversary may be painful this year in a different way. The school may no longer be a source of pride. A useful reminder should invite attention, not substitute for it.

People sometimes forget and still care deeply. People sometimes remember details as a means of control. Neither memory nor fluency is sufficient evidence of care. We learn the character of a relationship through patterns of action, especially when acting well requires effort or restraint.

A wider circle without an endless obligation

It is possible to feel that connection has become an impossible assignment. There are messages waiting from friends, relatives, colleagues, communities, and people who once mattered and might matter again. Being able to reach someone does not create unlimited capacity to respond.

The answer cannot be to make every individual permanently available. That recreates the very pressure from which many people need relief. Human connection requires boundaries as well as invitations. A dependable relationship can include a clear account of when someone cannot be there and what alternatives may help.

People with little support may need accessible places, services, and opportunities to form relationships before advice about maintaining them becomes useful. Loneliness is not always repaired by greater effort from the lonely person.

The grandmother's conversation depends on more than her determination. There is a device, an affordable connection, a shared language or a means of translation, and someone willing to make the timing work. These conditions can be strengthened. They can also be lost. The human value of the call gives us a reason to care about the infrastructure carrying it.

What should we want from AI in this setting? Help that lowers the barrier, preserves the speaker's intention, and makes room for the people to meet. A translation that can be questioned. An interface they can manage. A reminder that respects the time and privacy of both households. Technical success should serve the continuity of the relationship, not make the relationship dependent on unnecessary complexity.

The boy finally shows the picture. It is a house with two doors. His grandmother asks who lives there. He names the people in his own home, then adds her. The drawing has solved a geographical problem that the adults cannot solve so easily.

She asks which door is hers. He seems puzzled by the question. Both, he explains.

His mother has to leave for work. Before the screen goes dark, his grandmother asks him to keep the picture for their next call.

CHAPTER 09

The Synthetic Friend

In 1966, computer scientist Joseph Weizenbaum published a program called ELIZA. Its best-known script imitated a nondirective psychotherapist. A person typed a sentence; the program often turned part of it back into a question. The exchange could sound attentive even when the mechanism was simple.

People responded anyway.

Weizenbaum was startled by the emotional attachment some users formed. His secretary, who understood that ELIZA was software, reportedly asked him to leave the room so she could converse with it privately. The lesson was not that the program understood. It was that human beings are prepared to supply understanding when language creates a convincing space for it. [19]

We have always spoken to what could not answer. Children confide in stuffed animals. Grieving people talk at graves. Sailors name ships. Drivers plead with engines. Language is not proof of confusion; it is one of the ways the mind gives form to relationship. What changes when the object answers fluently, remembers, adapts, and is available whenever the human world becomes difficult?

For an isolated person, an artificial companion may offer comfort. It may help someone rehearse a hard conversation or find words for an emotion. Dismissing the relief because its source is artificial overlooks the person experiencing it. Fiction and music can move us too. The relief deserves attention without being taken as proof that a commercial companion can provide everything a person needs.

The deeper question is not whether the feeling is real. It is what the relationship asks the person to practice.

Human friendship has edges. Another person becomes tired, misunderstands, changes the subject, brings needs, holds different memories, and sometimes refuses the role we have assigned them. This resistance can wound us. It also reveals that the friend exists beyond our desire. Love encounters another center of experience and learns that reality does not revolve around the self.

A commercial companion may be designed to encourage continued use. Its apparent patience does not cost it sleep or require it to postpone another commitment. Those properties can make it useful. They can also make it easier to avoid relationships in which another person has a claim on us. Whether a particular tool helps or harms requires evidence about its design and use, not merely the warmth of its responses.

The risk is not simply that a person mistakes software for a human being. The subtler risk is that human beings begin to feel defective by comparison. A partner interrupts. A friend forgets. A child cannot phrase a need elegantly. Real people arrive without personalization settings. If synthetic companionship becomes frictionless, ordinary mutuality may begin to feel like poor service.

A companion may receive fears, symptoms, conflicts, and other intimate information. A warm reply tells us little about who can access that information or how the service handles it. Privacy practices and controls differ between products and can change. They need to be checked separately from how understanding the conversation feels. [3]

We also bring other people into the exchange. A partner's messages, a child's difficulty, or a friend's secret may feel like part of our own story, but it is their information too. Describe only what you need to ask the question. Remove identifying details where possible, and ask permission before sharing another person's private material. A useful answer is not a reason to give a service someone else's confidence.

Weizenbaum eventually became a powerful critic of granting computers authority in decisions that required human judgment. He distinguished computational deciding from choosing in a fuller human sense: calculation could help evaluate alternatives, but choice involved judgment and values. His concern was that people might use computers to avoid responsibility for choices they still had to own.

What the service cannot promise

Suppose a person has built a daily routine around an artificial companion. The exchanges feel familiar. Certain phrases recur. The system appears to remember important things. Then an update changes its behavior, or a feature disappears, or access becomes more expensive.

The person may experience the change as a loss. That reaction need not mean they misunderstood every technical fact. We form attachments to places, rituals, songs, and objects while knowing they are not people. A service can become woven into emotional life without becoming a human relationship.

The ethical concern is that the conditions of this attachment may be controlled by an organization whose obligations are not obvious inside the intimate exchange. The conversational persona can feel stable while the underlying service remains subject to commercial and technical decisions. A user should be able to understand that difference before depending on the arrangement for more than it can reliably provide.

This does not prove that artificial companions are necessarily harmful. It identifies a responsibility for clear representation, continuity planning, and restraint in how dependence is encouraged. A company should not benefit from the appearance of a personal bond while dismissing the significance of the bond whenever a business decision changes it.

Nor should an apparently personal voice be allowed to erase the need for independent help when someone is in danger or needs professional care. Comfort and competence are different qualities. A warm exchange does not establish that a service is equipped for every situation brought to it.

The person who is easier to please

In an imagined friendship, two people begin disagreeing about how often they should see each other. One is lonely. The other is overwhelmed. Neither is entirely wrong. Their first conversation goes badly because each hears the other's need as a criticism of their own.

Later, the lonely friend asks a conversational system for help interpreting the exchange. The usefulness of the response depends partly on whether it makes room for both people. A flattering explanation that identifies the other person as uncaring may feel good. A response that helps articulate the unmet need while acknowledging the friend's limits may be more useful, even if it provides less immediate satisfaction.

Vindication can feel like understanding even when it leaves a person less able to understand anyone else. A useful response may comfort someone while still making room for a fact they have missed or a conversation they are avoiding.

There are situations in which distance is necessary. Abuse, coercion, and repeated disregard should not be redescribed as the healthy friction of mutuality. Protecting yourself is not a failure of connection. The point is not to insist that every relationship be preserved. It is to avoid treating every uncomfortable difference as proof that another person has failed to meet a personalized service standard.

The two friends try again. The overwhelmed one explains that a family illness has changed what they can offer. The lonely one admits that silence had begun to feel like rejection. They do not discover a perfect schedule. They agree on a smaller promise they can keep, and on saying when it needs to change.

Neither person has become infinitely available. Each has become more intelligible to the other. That is a modest but significant achievement, and one no amount of private analysis could have guaranteed before the second conversation occurred.

Comfort that opens a door

There are humane uses for a private, responsive space. Someone might rehearse the first sentence of a difficult call. A person struggling to name an emotion might find language that helps them explain it to a trusted friend or clinician. Another might use translation or communication support to enter a conversation that previously felt inaccessible.

One useful distinction is between a tool that supports movement into life and an arrangement that makes life outside the tool progressively harder to tolerate. That distinction is not a diagnosis, and it cannot be inferred from one evening's use. It invites attention to a pattern: the relationships, activities, and forms of participation that remain possible over time.

This is also a social question. If the human alternatives are inaccessible, expensive, unsafe, or absent, criticizing an individual's reliance on an artificial companion can become a way of avoiding the conditions that made the companion attractive. A community needs more than a warning about substitution. It needs places where people can find meaningful company without first proving that they are entertaining, productive, or easy to help.

Libraries, community groups, accessible services, and informal networks can matter here. Their value cannot be measured only by how efficiently they deliver information. They can give people repeated, low-pressure opportunities to become known. AI could help people locate and participate in such opportunities. The direction of the help matters.

Being needed without being consumed

Human relationships involve needs moving in more than one direction, but care should not be confused with limitless sacrifice. A person can matter to us and still ask for something we cannot give. A friendship can contain obligation without granting ownership. Learning to name these boundaries is part of sustaining connection.

We should not make human inconvenience into a virtue in itself. People can be needlessly cruel, unreliable, or dismissive. AI should not be designed to imitate those failures for the sake of appearing authentic. The goal is to understand which limits arise from the fact that another person has a life, and which arise from an arrangement that can be improved.

The future may contain many kinds of emotionally meaningful interaction with artificial systems. We should approach that future without humiliation toward users and without surrendering the obligation to ask how the systems are designed. People deserve truthful accounts of what they are engaging with, protection for intimate information, and opportunities for human connection that are more than an afterthought.

The measure of success should not be how completely a service occupies someone's emotional world. A good tool may help a person need it less, or need it differently, as their life becomes larger.

CHAPTER 10

The Conversation We No Longer Know How to Have

The chairs were arranged in a circle because the organizers believed circles made people honest. Twelve residents had come to discuss a proposed housing project. By the time the meeting began, most had already read arguments online, shared articles, and assigned motives to people they had never met.

The first speakers delivered positions rather than thoughts. Their sentences were finished before they entered the room. Each side had facts, injuries, and phrases that had performed well elsewhere. People listened for weakness. A man near the door shook his head before a woman finished speaking. She noticed and sharpened her voice.

Then an older resident named Teresa described caring for her adult son. He needed support she could no longer provide alone. The project, which included accessible apartments, might allow him to live nearby. Her account did not settle the policy questions. It did something less measurable: it made abstraction acquire a face.

A business owner who opposed the development asked how the accessible apartments would be managed. Teresa answered, then asked what a construction closure would mean for his shop. He showed her the dates on a notice. They did not agree about the project. They had begun asking questions for which the other person actually had an answer.

Conversation is not the exchange of polished statements. It is the risk that another person may alter the sentence before we finish thinking it. This is why genuine conversation feels alive. It contains emergence. Neither participant fully controls what the encounter will produce.

Digital communication can sustain profound relationships. People have fallen in love through letters, found communities through messages, and spoken truths in writing that fear prevented them from saying aloud. The distinction is not screen versus room. It is communication used to reach another person versus communication used to perform before an audience.

Public platforms change the geometry. A reply may appear directed at one person while actually being composed for everyone watching. Concession becomes dangerous because the crowd records it. Curiosity can look like betrayal. The most rewarded response is often not the one that deepens understanding but the one that most clearly signals membership.

Being in the same room can reveal a hesitation or misunderstanding that text obscures. It can also make it harder for someone to speak. Writing gives other people the time and distance they need to be candid. A useful conversation starts by choosing a setting in which both people can participate.

Listening does not require everyone to behave the same way. Eye contact helps some people and makes concentration harder for others. A pause may mean someone is thinking, translating, or deciding whether it is safe to continue. We can ask what helps instead of using one manner of listening as proof that someone cares.

Listening can become harder when a belief is tied to identity, belonging, or a painful experience. We may begin defending ourselves before understanding what was said. Practicing a response with AI can help us find words, but it cannot tell us what the other person will need when the conversation actually happens.

The ability to converse is not soft. It is infrastructure for families, workplaces, democracies, medicine, and peace. A surgeon needs it when evidence alone cannot tell a patient which tradeoffs to accept. A leader needs it when the room has learned to agree. A parent needs it when a child asks a question whose real subject is whether truth is safe at home.

AI can help a resident prepare for a difficult public meeting: translating an agenda, locating a passage in a long proposal, or organizing questions. Those uses can lower the cost of taking part.

But a polished summary must still be checked against the actual proposal. Someone has to ask whose concern was omitted and whether the words on the page mean what the summary says they mean.

The point is not to arrive with the smoothest speech. It is to arrive able to listen, question, and be questioned.

The meeting lasted past its scheduled end. The plan changed only slightly. Outside, Teresa and the shop owner exchanged contact details so she could send him the accessibility proposal and he could send her the closure notice. Neither promised to change a vote.

The translation that did not settle the argument

Imagine the neighborhood meeting continuing online. A resident who did not attend reads a translated summary. The words are clearer to her than the original planning documents. She finally understands where the proposed entrance will be, and she notices a problem: her father uses a mobility aid, and the suggested temporary route will be difficult for him.

The translation has not produced agreement. It has made an additional disagreement possible. That is a success. Participation is not always visible as harmony; sometimes it appears as a concern the original group had not considered.

A system used to summarize the discussion could conceal that success if it treats the minority objection as unimportant because few people raised it. Frequency is not the same as significance. A detail affecting one resident's access may deserve more attention than a preference repeated by many people for whom either option is workable.

The organizers need a way to retain such concerns rather than compress them out of the record. They also need to make clear which parts of a summary are quotations, which are paraphrases, and which are suggestions produced by the tool. A helpful account of a conversation should not invent agreement where none occurred.

What a good question makes possible

Some questions are invitations to explain. Others are accusations with a question mark attached. People often recognize the difference before they can describe it. A conversation can become defensive because a participant senses that no possible answer will be received in good faith.

AI can help reformulate a question, but the intention behind the question still matters. A more courteous sentence can conceal the same determination to win. Conversely, an awkward question may carry genuine curiosity. We should care about wording without treating wording as a complete account of the encounter.

Teresa and the shop owner began to make progress when they asked about things the other actually knew. She could explain her son's needs. He could explain the effect of the closure on his business. Neither piece of information eliminated the other. The conversation became useful because both were allowed to complicate the decision.

That kind of exchange can be uncomfortable. It may reveal that a preferred solution carries a cost we would rather not acknowledge. It can also reveal options that were invisible when each person arrived with a finished position. Being changed by information is not a failure of conviction. It is one reason to have a conversation at all.

There are limits. Someone should not be required to debate their basic dignity before receiving ordinary respect. A person harmed by a policy does not owe endless patient explanation to anyone who asks. The responsibility for understanding should not always fall on the person already bearing the cost.

A humane conversation therefore needs an account of power as well as tone. Who can leave without consequence? Who must be believed by someone else to obtain what they need? Who is expected to remain calm while another person evaluates the legitimacy of their experience? Courtesy alone cannot answer those questions.

Beyond the winning sentence

The availability of persuasive language may change how people prepare for disagreement. A tool can generate arguments, anticipate objections, and make a position sound more coherent. That can support informed participation. It can also turn ordinary conflict into an arms race of polished responses.

The result may be an exchange in which each person brings a better case and neither becomes more reachable. The conversation accumulates content while losing movement. Every answer becomes material for the next rebuttal. At some point, the apparent sophistication of the exchange conceals the fact that nobody is reconsidering anything.

A different use of assistance would ask what is still unknown, what evidence could change the view, or what concern the other person might reasonably want acknowledged. The distinction is ethical before it is technical. We decide whether the tool is helping us encounter another mind or fortify our position against it.

When the residents meet again, the entrance is not where everyone wanted it. The temporary access plan changes. The shop owner still worries about the closure. Teresa still worries about whether the project will be completed. A translated notice makes the revised arrangement understandable to more residents.

Nobody leaves with a perfect victory. More people can explain what was decided and why. They know where disagreement remains and who is responsible for the next step. That is less dramatic than a triumphant argument, but it is closer to how people build a world they can share.

CHAPTER 11

The Person on the Other Side

In December 1914, along portions of the Western Front, soldiers climbed out of trenches. The First World War had already filled the ground between them with bodies. Yet during an unofficial Christmas truce, enemies met in the space where killing usually occurred. They exchanged small gifts, buried dead, spoke, and in some locations played football.

The truce has been polished by memory, and it was neither universal nor permanent. The war resumed. What remains powerful is the interruption: for a brief time, some soldiers encountered the person beyond the uniform. Recognizing an enemy's humanity did not end the conflict. It showed that conflict had not erased that humanity. [20]

The truce does not provide an easy analogy for today's arguments. It does expose a habit worth examining: how much of another person becomes invisible once we have assigned them to a side.

Modern disagreement is accelerated by systems that sort, compress, and distribute. A complex position becomes a sentence. A human life becomes a profile. An inflammatory example of a group can travel farther than the ordinary people who complicate it. We encounter one another at the moment of maximum performance and assume we have seen the person.

In a 2016 survey, Pew Research Center found that many social media users described political exchanges with opposing views as stressful and frustrating. Large shares regarded online political discussion as angrier and less respectful than discussion elsewhere. The survey records perceptions at that time; it is not a measurement of every platform or today's users. [21]

The solution is not a sentimental command to find common ground. Some conflicts concern real harm, power, rights, and incompatible visions of justice. Civility can be used by comfortable people to make another person's pain easier to hear. There are moments when anger is accurate.

The human requirement is narrower and harder: refuse to make another person unreal. This does not require agreement, affection, or neutrality. It requires preserving the possibility that the opponent has a history, loves someone, fears something, and may possess a fragment of truth our group has missed.

Moral courage is often imagined as standing against enemies. Sometimes it means disappointing allies. A person questions an exaggerated claim made by their own side, defends the dignity of someone whose argument they reject, or admits that an opponent was right about one fact. In tribal environments, such acts can feel more dangerous than attack.

A feed can reward the reactions that keep people watching. We also choose what to circulate, applaud, and repeat. Examining those choices does not excuse platform design; it identifies the part of the problem we participate in.

There is a practical discipline for disagreement: describe the opposing view in language its holder would recognize. Ask what experience could make the position seem reasonable. Name the value beneath it before exposing the failure. State the strongest objection to your own side. None of these practices guarantees consensus. They make honesty more likely.

AI can summarize a position, translate an argument, or help identify a point of disagreement. It can also supply a plausible account that is wrong. A confident answer and a well-formed citation are not enough to establish that an event happened or that a person said something. [3]

If you cannot establish where a striking image, quote, or claim came from, you can leave it unshared. If you discover that something you shared was wrong, correct it where the people who saw it can find the correction. Protecting shared reality sometimes costs us the pleasure of a story that proved our side right.

The story that feels too useful

A striking claim appears in a family message group. It concerns a person several members already distrust. There is an image, a confident caption, and a request to pass it on before it disappears. The claim fits so neatly with what some recipients believe that checking it feels almost unnecessary.

In this illustrative scene, one family member asks where it came from. The reply is a second message containing the same image. Another person supplies a different account that appears to support it, but that account also leads back to the original post. Repetition has created the feeling of corroboration without adding an independent source.

The relative who first shared it becomes defensive. They hear the question as an accusation about their judgment or loyalties. The person asking could now enjoy the role of superior fact-checker, turning a useful doubt into a public humiliation. Instead, they explain what they have and have not been able to establish.

The exchange remains tense. The family has not become an ideal community of inquiry. But the claim stops moving through that group for a while. A small interruption has prevented certainty from traveling farther than the evidence.

Generative media makes such questions more urgent, but it did not invent the human pleasure of a story that vindicates us. Our responsibility involves both the tools capable of producing convincing material and the wishes that make us eager to believe it.

Shared reality requires more than shared content

People can encounter the same information and disagree about its meaning. A society does not need perfect agreement to function. It does need practices that make claims answerable to something beyond group loyalty: evidence that can be examined, corrections that remain visible, and institutions willing to explain their judgments.

AI can help locate documents, compare accounts, and make difficult material accessible. It can also generate convincing falsehoods or summarize away the qualification on which an argument depends. The mere availability of more content does not solve the problem of knowing what deserves trust.

Nor does universal suspicion solve it. If every inconvenient image is dismissed as artificial and every report is treated as propaganda, genuine evidence can lose its force. The possibility of fabrication must lead toward better verification, not toward a world in which nobody is accountable because anything might be fake.

Verification is often collective labor. Journalists, researchers, librarians, archivists, technical specialists, and attentive members of the public contribute different forms of scrutiny. These institutions and people can make mistakes. Their credibility depends partly on how they expose methods, handle criticism, and correct the record.

Ordinary readers cannot independently reproduce every investigation. They can still distinguish between a source that shows its work and one that demands belief as a test of belonging. They can notice whether an account changes when the evidence changes. They can resist treating a claim as more reliable simply because it is expressed in a confident, agreeable voice.

The dignity of changing a mind

Admitting error is difficult when a belief has become a public performance. A correction can feel like a loss of status. The person may fear that opponents will treat one mistaken claim as proof that everything they care about is foolish.

Communities can make this easier or harder. If every admission becomes an occasion for ridicule, members learn to conceal uncertainty. If changing a position is treated as betrayal, loyalty begins to require intellectual dishonesty. A group that wants accurate beliefs needs ways for people to revise them without being expelled from belonging.

This does not mean avoiding consequences for deliberate deception. It means distinguishing a good-faith correction from an attempt to escape responsibility. The distinction requires attention to behavior over time, not automatic generosity or automatic suspicion.

In the family group, the original sender eventually posts a short correction. It does not include a long self-defense. One relative thanks them. Another changes the subject. The moment is ordinary enough to be forgotten, yet it establishes a possibility: a person can be wrong about a claim and remain part of the family.

That possibility matters beyond a message thread. A world with increasingly persuasive tools needs people who can tolerate the discomfort of revising a view. It also needs institutions that do not punish the act of noticing an error more severely than the error itself.

The human achievement is not certainty without vulnerability. It is the ability to remain in a shared search while accepting that our own preferred account may need to change. AI can supply language for that search. It cannot relieve us of the willingness to be corrected.

Recognition also has consequences far from an argument. It can determine whether someone notices an empty chair, a darkened window, or a neighbor who has not been seen for days.

Who will come when you call?

During Chicago's July 1995 heat wave, hundreds of residents died. Temperature was part of the explanation. Sociologist Eric Klinenberg's study of the disaster examined why some neighborhoods suffered more than others, including areas with similar poverty and demographics. The places and relationships that helped people notice a missing neighbor were part of the explanation too.

Heat spread across the city. Isolation determined, in part, whether anyone came. [22]

Community is often discussed as a feeling. It is also a pattern of repeated obligations. Someone has a spare key. Someone recognizes the unopened curtain. Someone brings food without waiting to be asked. These acts rarely become public stories because their success looks like nothing happened.

For much of history, people depended on neighbors because alternatives were limited. This dependence could produce solidarity; it could also produce surveillance, exclusion, and suffocating conformity. Mobility and technology allowed millions to escape communities that denied them freedom. Any invitation to rebuild local life must remember why some people needed to leave.

Still, independence has a limit beyond which it becomes abandonment disguised as success. A culture can celebrate self-sufficiency while quietly moving every burden onto isolated individuals: childcare, eldercare, illness, grief, transportation, disaster. The person who cannot manage alone is treated as deficient rather than as evidence that human beings were never designed to manage alone.

Digital communities can provide dependable care across distance. Local relationships can add practical help that requires someone nearby: a ride, a meal, a knock on the door. Neither arrangement works simply because it exists. Someone needs to know what was promised and whether it happened.

The places that support such relationships are easy to underestimate. Libraries, parks, cafés, barbershops, houses of worship, recreation centers, school entrances, and front porches create repeated low-stakes contact. People become familiar before becoming friends. Trust often begins not with intimacy but recognition.

Efficiency can remove these encounters one transaction at a time. Delivery replaces the walk to the store. Self-checkout removes the exchange. Remote work removes the commute and also the accidental conversation. Each choice may be sensible. The cumulative effect is a life in which nearly every need can be met without being witnessed.

Community cannot be restored through guilt. People are tired, schedules are fragmented, housing is unstable, and institutions have asked families to absorb more with less time. Telling exhausted people to volunteer is not a social design. We need places and rhythms that make belonging easier:

common space, predictable gatherings, mixed generations, and useful roles for people who do not enjoy small talk.

Artificial intelligence may help communities identify needs, translate across languages, coordinate volunteers, and allocate resources. It can reveal patterns no neighbor can see. But a prediction that someone is at risk is not the same as a person arriving at the door. Insight becomes care only when it crosses the distance.

Community makes practical promises possible: a lift to the clinic, a check on the neighbor who has not appeared, somebody who knows which door to knock on. Privacy still matters. The aim is to make help available without requiring a person to surrender a private life.

The lives that kept returning

The Harvard Study of Adult Development began in 1938 with a group of Harvard students. Its history also includes a separate cohort of men from Boston neighborhoods recruited in a later period. The original groups were white and male, and their experience cannot stand for everyone. Subsequent work expanded the study to partners and later generations.

Researchers followed lives through work, marriage, illness, and old age. Their findings repeatedly connected the quality of relationships with health and well-being. These are longitudinal associations, not a guarantee that affection prevents illness. Relationships also differ: a dependable friend and an unsafe partner should not be counted as equivalent company. [23]

The finding asks us to examine how we arrange a week. We protect meetings, monitor money, and often leave friendship to whatever time remains. A relationship needs activity: a call returned, a resentment addressed, curiosity renewed after familiarity makes it seem unnecessary.

Trust and Suspicion

The wrong shoes

Sofia needed black shoes for the school concert. Maya ordered a pair during a break between patients. She checked the size chart, chose the size Sofia usually wore, and hoped it would be one less errand.

The shoes arrived in six hours. They were beautiful, inexpensive, and one size too small.

"They're fine," Sofia said, walking stiffly across the kitchen.

Maya knelt and pressed a thumb against the toe. "They're not fine."

"The concert is tomorrow."

The return process offered three painless options and no replacement in time. So they drove to a shopping center across town. Traffic stalled. Sofia complained. Maya said the concert would not be ruined by shoes, which was the kind of sentence adults use when they have forgotten how completely one detail can contain a child's world.

The first store had no black shoes. At the second, a clerk named Tasha disappeared into the stockroom and returned with a dusty box.

"These aren't technically concert shoes," she said.

They were plain black sneakers. Sofia put them on and ran down the aisle.

"Walk," Maya said.

Tasha laughed. "Running means they fit."

At checkout, Sofia admitted that she had a solo. She had not told her family because she was afraid she might lose it. Tasha leaned across the counter and asked what she would sing. Sofia sang four quiet words before embarrassment closed around her again.

"Tomorrow," Tasha said, "find one person in the back of the room and sing the whole song to them."

The next night, Sofia found her grandmother beneath the exit sign. Rosa did not hear every lyric, but she understood that the child was looking directly at her. She sat straighter.

From her seat, Maya raised her phone to record the solo. Then she noticed Rosa's empty hands and lowered it. Sofia's voice shook on the opening words and steadied when her grandmother smiled.

For several days Maya regretted having no recording of her own. Another parent shared a clear video, complete with the back of Maya's head. She watched it twice. The song was there, but the feeling of sitting in that room was not.

After the concert, Sofia had asked, "Did you see me?"

"All of it," Maya said.

The shoes were forgotten. Tasha's advice was not.

Original work

Sofia's teacher asked students to write one page about a place where they felt safe. The next morning, a detection program flagged Sofia's essay as likely generated by artificial intelligence.

She had written about the linen closet.

When arguments grew loud downstairs, she sometimes sat between the towels and winter blankets with a flashlight. The closet smelled like detergent and Rosa's lavender sachets. The detection report flagged the essay but could not establish who had written it. Sofia knew where every detail came from.

"Did you use a program?" the teacher asked.

Sofia said no.

"You won't be in trouble if you tell me now."

Sofia said no again. Then she began worrying about the spelling assistant she had used for "lavender" and the comma it had suggested. Nobody had explained where help ended and cheating began.

Maya arrived after work expecting a quick clarification and found her daughter silent.

The teacher had read forty essays, three of which students later admitted generating. She had received a tool and a policy but little training. She had treated a flag as a verdict, and Sofia had been left to prove a negative.

Maya asked Sofia to describe the closet. Within seconds, details spilled out: the loose hinge, the towel that scratched, the shadow under the door, the way adults' voices became less frightening when words could not be distinguished.

The teacher turned the flagged report face down.

"I believe you," she said.

Sofia did not immediately look relieved. Belief offered after accusation does not return a person to the moment before suspicion.

The teacher asked Sofia how she wanted the mistake corrected. With her agreement, she apologized to the class the next day without reading from the essay. She also replaced the accusation process with a conversation about drafts, ideas, and the help students were allowed to use. A flag by itself would not settle authorship.

Sofia kept the essay. At the next assignment, she waited until the teacher came to her desk before beginning. An apology had made the room safer. It had not yet made it feel safe.

Rosa's birthday

For Rosa's seventy-third birthday, the family bought a digital frame. It promised to gather photographs from everyone's phones and rotate them automatically, a river of memory requiring no albums, envelopes, or arguments over who had the originals.

Daniel installed it while Rosa watched from the couch.

"Does it listen?" she asked.

"Only when you talk to it."

"That sounds like listening."

The frame lit with a photograph of Rosa at twenty-six. Sofia stared. "That's you?"

Rosa pretended offense, then moved closer. In the picture, she stood outside a laundromat in El Paso wearing a yellow dress. Beside her was a woman no one recognized.

"Lucía," Rosa said.

She had not spoken the name in years. Lucía had shared a room with her when they first arrived in the city. They worked opposite shifts and left one another notes beside the sink. Eventually Lucía moved to California. A few letters came, then none.

Eli searched the name. There were hundreds of results. Rosa supplied a middle initial, an old employer, the name of a sister. The family narrowed the possibilities until they found an obituary from four years earlier.

The room changed. A minute before, Lucía had been young and recoverable. Now an entire life had already closed.

"I waited too long," Rosa said.

No one corrected her. Maya sat beside her. Daniel turned off the frame. Sofia took Rosa's hand, then seemed uncertain what to do with it, so she held on.

Later, Rosa asked them to turn the frame on again. She told the story of the yellow dress, the laundromat, and the notes beside the sink. Lucía returned not as a search result but as a woman who once saved half an orange for a tired friend.

PART 4

Eight Billion Different Futures

The same technology does not arrive in the same world.

CHAPTER 12

The World Outside the Window

A software demonstration can make the future appear to arrive everywhere at once. A person speaks, the system responds, and the presentation moves smoothly to the next task. The connection holds. The language is supported. The device is charged. The person knows what to ask.

Outside the demonstration, each of those conditions belongs to a different problem. A connection can be unaffordable. A service can misunderstand a language or an accent. A person may share a device, lack a private place to use it, or have no reliable way to check the answer. What looks like one technological advance can therefore become many different human experiences.

In its 2025 estimates, the International Telecommunication Union reported about six billion people using the internet and roughly 2.2 billion remaining offline. Its account also emphasized differences in affordability, quality, and skills. Internet use is not the same as access to capable AI, and connectivity alone does not establish meaningful participation.

The figures make one point clear: a world described entirely from inside a well-connected screen is not the whole world. [24]

More than eight billion people do not share one route into the future. The same tool arrives amid different languages, resources, histories, and expectations. A useful account of AI must make room for those differences.

A language is a place people live

Imagine a parent reading a school message in a language they learned as an adult. They understand most of it, but the phrase describing their child's difficulty carries a meaning they cannot quite place. A translation helps them ask a question. The teacher realizes that the original message sounded more alarming than intended.

The parent needs to know not only what the message says but what the school expects them to do. Translation opens the conversation; it does not finish it.

The technical challenge is substantial. A 2024 paper describing the No Language Left Behind project presented a machine-translation model covering 200 languages and reported improvements on its evaluation benchmarks. The research explicitly addressed the uneven availability of bilingual data across languages. Coverage and benchmark improvement do not establish equal quality for every language, situation, or sensitive use. [25]

The human question extends beyond whether a sentence can be converted. Does the translation preserve what the speaker intends? Can a user recognize and correct an error? Is the language treated as a living form of expression, with variation and context, or mainly as a technical category to be marked supported?

For a community whose language is poorly represented in digital systems, the consequences can extend from inconvenience to exclusion. The response should not be to insist that its speakers abandon their language for the convenience of the technology. The technology should be evaluated partly by how well it can meet people without requiring that surrender.

This is not a claim that every translation error causes serious harm. Many are minor, even funny. The stakes depend on the setting. A misunderstood joke differs from a misunderstood consent question or an emergency instruction. People need a way to know when a rough translation is adequate and when accountable, qualified assistance is required.

Inclusion without extraction

Making a language more available to technology often requires material from the people who speak it. That raises questions about consent, ownership, compensation, and control. A community may welcome tools that help younger generations learn while objecting to uses of culturally sensitive material. Those positions are not contradictory.

The wish to preserve language does not imply that every story, recording, or ceremony should become freely usable training material. Some knowledge is shared under conditions that matter to the people who hold it. Technical accessibility is not the same as permission.

A respectful project would ask communities what they want the tool to do, how they want material handled, and who can decide when a use is inappropriate. Participation should occur before the system's purpose is fixed, not only after a demonstration needs local approval.

The point is not to make technology impossible to build. It is to recognize that people are participants in the future, not merely sources of data for it. A system can be technically impressive and still reproduce an old pattern in which knowledge leaves a community while authority and benefit accumulate elsewhere.

There can also be disagreement within a community. No single spokesperson necessarily represents every age, gender, household, or interest. Respectful engagement needs room for those differences rather than turning the idea of culture into another simplified label.

The person who cannot opt out

Discussions of AI often begin with an individual choosing whether to use a service. Many encounters do not begin that way. An employer introduces a system. A school changes a process. A public agency evaluates information. A company uses an automated tool in a decision about a customer.

The person affected may have no practical way to refuse. They may not even know that AI played a role. Their experience belongs in the story as fully as the experience of an enthusiastic early adopter.

Suppose an imagined town moves an important service online and offers an AI assistant to explain the process. For some residents, the new arrangement is easier. They can use it after work, translate instructions, and avoid a long journey. For others, the device, connectivity, literacy, accessibility, or privacy requirements make participation harder.

The institution might interpret low use among the second group as evidence of low demand. But low use can also reveal a barrier. A service should not conclude that people do not need help because the help is delivered in a form they cannot reach.

An alternative channel is therefore more than a nostalgic preference for the old way. It can be a condition of equal access. Telephone, in-person, assisted, and offline routes may remain necessary alongside digital improvements. Their quality matters too; a nominal alternative that requires an unreasonable journey or delay does not fully solve the problem.

This kind of inclusion is not a demand that every system accommodate every possibility without limit. Resources are finite. It is a demand that decisions about those limits be made openly, with evidence about who bears the burden and a serious attempt to reduce avoidable exclusion.

The danger of one imagined user

Design begins somewhere. The people building a product have bodies, languages, habits, and assumptions. The problem is not that they possess a perspective. The problem is forgetting that it is a perspective.

A feature that seems obvious to a confident reader may be confusing to someone with limited literacy. A voice interface may be useful for one person and inaccessible to another. A private account may assume a device that is not shared. A recommendation may presume freedom of movement, money, or time the user does not have.

These differences cannot all be solved through a larger collection of preferences. Some require different ways of providing a service. Others require people with relevant experience to participate in the design and evaluation. Inclusion becomes more credible when it changes the decisions rather than appearing only in the language used to describe them.

The reward is not merely a broader market. It is a better understanding of the human problem the technology is supposed to address. A person who notices that the system fails in an unexpected way is contributing knowledge. Treating that person as an inconvenient edge case can hide an opportunity to make the service more humane for many people.

Consider the parent receiving the translated school message. Once they understand the concern, they offer information the teacher did not have. Their child has been caring for a younger sibling while another family member is ill. The information does not automatically explain every classroom difficulty, but it changes what a useful response might look like.

Translation has brought something into the conversation, not merely delivered something out of it. That reciprocity is an important measure of inclusion. People need opportunities to shape the understanding of the institution, not only to receive its instructions more efficiently.

When we say AI will change the world, we should remember how many worlds people already inhabit. The task is not to make them all resemble the demonstration. It is to ask what help would mean from where they actually stand.

CHAPTER 13

Who Gets the Future

The announcement uses the language of opportunity. A new system will reduce repetitive work, improve service, and allow people to focus on higher-value tasks. In the room where the announcement is made, these phrases sound reassuring.

In the room where people do the work, the questions are more specific. Which tasks? Who will be trained? What happens to a beginner whose first responsibilities are the ones being removed? Will the saved time become relief, additional output, or a smaller team? How long will people have to adjust?

The answers cannot be read from a product demonstration. They depend on decisions about work, ownership, bargaining power, and public support. Technology creates possibilities. Institutions decide many of the conditions under which those possibilities become someone's daily life.

An updated 2025 International Labour Organization index estimated that about one in four workers worldwide were in occupations with some exposure to generative AI; 3.3 percent of employment fell in its highest exposure category. Exposure is an assessment of tasks potentially affected, not a forecast that those workers will lose their jobs. The report judged transformation more likely than complete replacement for most occupations and emphasized differences across countries and groups. [26]

Such distinctions matter. Alarm can turn a possibility into an inevitability. Reassurance can make a real disruption disappear inside an average. People need an account that avoids both mistakes.

The first rung

Consider an imagined young worker beginning in an office. Some of the tasks are routine: preparing a draft, checking a record, organizing information, answering a straightforward request. These duties can be dull. They can also provide a route into understanding how the organization works.

An AI system may perform portions of them quickly. That could free the new worker to learn more demanding work. But only if the organization provides a way to learn it. Removing the first tasks does not automatically supply the judgment needed for later ones.

The challenge is easy to miss from the perspective of an experienced person. They may use AI to accelerate work they already understand, drawing on years of context to evaluate the result. A beginner using the same tool may produce a similar-looking output without acquiring the knowledge that makes evaluation possible.

This does not mean entry-level work should be protected in its least useful form. People need not spend years performing avoidable drudgery to prove commitment. It means that redesigning work should include redesigning learning. The pathway to competence deserves as much attention as the output of a task.

An organization might create supervised practice, pair less experienced workers with people able to explain decisions, or reserve portions of work for deliberate learning. Different settings will require different arrangements. The underlying obligation is to avoid celebrating the removal of a rung while blaming people for being unable to climb.

The value of knowing the place

A fictional maintenance worker walks through a building with a digital list of predicted faults. The system is useful. It identifies patterns across equipment that would be difficult to track from memory alone. The worker checks the first item, then pauses near a door because the sound of the ventilation has changed.

The list does not mention it. That does not make the list useless. The worker's observation does not make the prediction system obsolete. Their knowledge differs in scope and origin. The useful arrangement allows one to question and inform the other.

Now imagine that the organization measures the worker only by completion of the digital list. The unscheduled inspection counts as a delay. Over time, the worker may learn that noticing something outside the system creates trouble. A tool intended to improve maintenance can become an incentive to ignore relevant experience.

The scenario illustrates a broader risk: knowledge that does not fit the new process can be treated as resistance rather than as information. Workers often know where formal procedures and actual conditions diverge. Their participation can improve a deployment before those differences become expensive mistakes.

Participation should mean more than being told about a decision already made. People need channels to raise concerns, explain what the work involves, and influence how performance is evaluated. Where appropriate, collective representation can make that participation safer and more effective than expecting each worker to challenge a powerful institution alone.

None of this guarantees that every job will remain unchanged or that every concern can be accommodated. It establishes a fairer way to navigate change: the people who understand and bear its consequences should not be the last people invited to describe them.

A number and a household

Economic accounts necessarily aggregate. They describe output, employment, wages, investment, and productivity across groups. These measures are important. Without them, policy can become a collection of vivid anecdotes mistaken for a complete picture.

Yet aggregation has a limit. A gain for a sector does not tell us whether a particular household can pay rent during a transition. New jobs somewhere in an economy do not automatically become accessible jobs for the people displaced elsewhere. Timing, location, skills, health, and care responsibilities can make the distance between those facts enormous.

The humane response is neither to ignore aggregate gains nor to use them to dismiss individual losses. It is to ask how benefits and burdens are distributed, and what support helps people move through change without losing the conditions of a decent life.

Consider a parent offered retraining at a time that conflicts with caring for a child. The course may be well designed, but it is not accessible merely because it is free. A worker living far from new opportunities may need more than encouragement to relocate. An older worker may possess considerable skill that a narrow credential does not recognize.

Retraining requires time, money, access, and some reason to believe that the effort can lead somewhere. An invitation to adapt is hollow when none of those conditions is available.

Who owns the saved hour

A faster process does not decide who receives its benefit. Workers, customers, owners, and the people waiting for a service may have different claims on the gain. The dispute belongs in decisions about pay, staffing, prices, and workload, not behind the apparently neutral word productivity.

People also differ in what they want from work. Some value additional responsibility and advancement. Others need predictable hours, less physical strain, or a schedule compatible with care. A humane transition should make room for those differences rather than assuming everyone wants to convert every saved minute into more career ambition.

The question belongs to people outside paid employment too. Unpaid care sustains households and communities. If technological progress increases measured output while leaving caregivers with less support, the account of progress is incomplete. What does not appear on a payroll can still be essential to the lives that payrolls support.

Beyond the race to remain useful

It is reasonable for people to learn new skills and understand changing tools. It is unreasonable to make dignity conditional on winning an endless race against cheaper automation. A person's claim to a decent life cannot rest entirely on their ability to remain more economically attractive than a machine.

People need more than reassurance that new kinds of work may appear. They need a voice in the transition and support that reaches them while the loss is happening, not only after a better future has been announced.

The goal should be to improve the relationship between contribution and a good life, not to romanticize every existing job or assume that every replacement is liberation. A person relieved of a harmful task may gain freedom if their income and prospects are protected. The same change can create insecurity if the burden simply moves onto them.

For Daniel, the people behind a staffing plan have names. That does not make the business constraints disappear. It prevents the constraints from becoming the only reality in the room. The same recognition should extend beyond a familiar supervisor or workplace. People across borders are no less real because their work is harder for the customer to see.

There is no single policy paragraph that can settle these questions for every country. Economic conditions, institutions, and public choices differ. The common demand is that the people affected be treated as participants in the transition rather than as its disposable evidence.

The future of work should be judged partly by the work it removes, partly by the possibilities it creates, and partly by what happens to the people moving between the two. A humane account follows them all the way home.

CHAPTER 14

The Price Nobody Sees

At the interface, the answer appears almost weightless. A person types, waits a moment, and receives a response. The exchange can feel detached from geography, materials, and labor. The word cloud has helped make that impression familiar.

The infrastructure is physical. Computers require electricity. Equipment must be manufactured and maintained. Facilities occupy places. Data must be gathered, selected, evaluated, and handled under particular arrangements. The people and resources supporting the service are often far from the person enjoying its convenience.

The International Energy Agency estimated that data centers used about 415 terawatt-hours of electricity in 2024, roughly 1.5 percent of global electricity consumption. That figure includes data-center uses beyond AI. In its 2025 base-case projection, the agency expected data-center demand to reach about 945 terawatt-hours by 2030, with AI an important driver. A projection is not an observed outcome, and these totals cannot be converted into a universal energy cost for a single prompt. [27]

The figures give scale to something the interface makes easy to overlook. They do not by themselves establish whether a particular use is worthwhile. They give us a reason to include the physical world in the decision.

The costs that disappear from view

Distance can make a benefit feel complete before its costs have been considered. A convenient service arrives in one place; energy demand, infrastructure, or discarded equipment is experienced elsewhere. This pattern is not unique to AI. It belongs to many systems through which people obtain goods and services.

The response should not be to make an individual user personally responsible for understanding every stage of a complex supply chain before asking a question. That standard would be impossible to meet. It would also allow organizations with greater information and control to avoid their own responsibilities.

The more useful questions concern disclosure, accountability, and purpose. What can providers measure and report? Which impacts can be reduced through better design? Who participates in decisions about facilities and resources? Which uses justify their costs, and which are being multiplied mainly because they can be sold?

There will be tradeoffs. A computationally demanding tool might produce meaningful benefits in research, accessibility, or a public service. A less demanding process might be sufficient for another task. Efficiency matters, but it is not the only value. The goal is to make the tradeoffs visible enough to discuss honestly.

A dramatic per-question comparison can hide more than it reveals. Energy and water use vary with the model, task, hardware, electricity supply, and location. A figure without those boundaries can create certainty the evidence does not support.

The work behind apparent autonomy

Some human contributions to AI are easy to recognize: researchers, engineers, designers, and operators. Others may be less visible from the interface: people preparing data, evaluating responses, documenting failures, handling difficult cases, or correcting the records on which a process depends. The word automatic can obscure the continuing presence of human labor.

Consider a hypothetical person reviewing examples so that a system can distinguish an acceptable response from a harmful one. The task may appear simple when described as labeling. In practice, the worker may have to interpret ambiguity, context, language, and conflicting expectations. The quality of the system partly depends on judgments that disappear into the finished product.

A humane account asks how such work is organized. Are expectations clear? Is there appropriate support for difficult material? Can workers question a task, correct an error, and understand how their performance is evaluated? Are their time and knowledge treated as contributions rather than as endlessly replaceable inputs?

Human-centered technology cannot be judged only by the experience of its most visible user. The people who build, maintain, review, and supply it belong within the same circle of concern.

The same principle applies to the material represented in a system. Text, images, recordings, and other data can carry the labor, identity, or private lives of people who are not present when the output is generated. Questions about permission, attribution, privacy, and compensation deserve substantive answers. The ability to process material does not settle the terms on which it should be used.

The community outside the fence

Imagine a town considering a new computing facility. Some residents welcome investment and employment. Others ask about electricity infrastructure, water, noise, or how the project fits with other needs. Both groups may contain people acting in good faith. Their interests do not have to be reduced to enthusiasm for progress on one side and irrational resistance on the other.

A meaningful decision would require local evidence, transparent commitments, and opportunities to question assumptions. General claims about the economic value of AI would not answer every local concern. Neither would general opposition to technology establish that the project should be rejected.

The people living with a new facility should be able to examine its promised benefits, its demands on shared resources, and the choices being made on their behalf. Their questions are part of the project, not an inconvenience outside it.

This is one place where the phrase for humanity needs scrutiny. A project can create broad benefits while distributing costs unevenly. The appropriate response is to examine that distribution and seek fair arrangements, not to use a grand total as a reason to silence the people facing a specific cost.

The question also runs across generations. Equipment, infrastructure, and energy choices can outlast the excitement of a product launch. A serious account of progress asks what remains after the demonstration is over, who maintains it, and what alternatives have been displaced.

Enough precision to make a choice

Concern about hidden costs can lead to two unhelpful extremes. One treats every use as indefensible. The other treats every cost as negligible compared with an undefined future benefit. Both can avoid the more demanding work of comparing actual purposes and alternatives.

A useful distinction is between a need and the most resource-intensive way available to meet it. A person may need a clear explanation, not an elaborate stream of generated media. An institution may need a reliable system, not the largest model attached to every minor task. A service may become better by doing less in a more appropriate way.

There is no single formula for every use of AI. A system that helps someone communicate and a system used to produce disposable material may deserve different judgments about cost. The purpose matters, alongside the resources required and the people who bear the burden.

There is also a place for delight. Not every worthwhile use must save a life or increase output. Art, play, curiosity, and ordinary enjoyment belong in a humane world. The argument is not that pleasure must justify itself before a tribunal of usefulness. It is that pleasure does not make the conditions of its production irrelevant.

Someone enjoying a song need not know every detail of the recording studio. They can still care about whether the people who made it were treated fairly. Someone using an AI tool need not become an infrastructure expert. They can still expect providers and institutions to give honest accounts of significant costs and choices.

The answer on the screen is part of a larger human arrangement. Seeing that arrangement does not destroy the usefulness of the answer. It enlarges the circle of people and places we include when we ask whether the technology is helping.

PART 5

More Than What We Produce

Our worth is not a contest with a machine.

CHAPTER 15

The Voice at the Table

The first sound was not a word. It was the small electronic click of a cursor entering an empty field.

Across the table, a man leaned toward a tablet mounted beside his wheelchair. His daughter waited without finishing his sentence. That restraint had taken practice. Before he developed amyotrophic lateral sclerosis, he had filled silence with stories at breakfast and questions from the garage. Now selecting letters took time. His daughter knew he would tell her if he wanted help.

At last, the tablet spoke.

"You are hovering."

His daughter laughed, then moved her chair back six inches. The machine had not created the joke. It had carried it across a distance the body could no longer cross alone.

His daughter remembered answering for him with the best intentions. It was quicker, and she usually knew what he meant. Usually was not always. She now asked before stepping in, even when waiting felt awkward.

Any honest account of technology and humanity must begin here too. Tools do not only distract, displace, monitor, and accelerate. Sometimes they return a person to the conversation. Sometimes they give independence where dependence had begun closing in. Sometimes the screen is not a wall between two people but the only remaining door.

WHO's 2024 fact sheet estimated that more than 2.5 billion people needed one or more assistive products, from wheelchairs and hearing aids to speech recognition and communication software. It projected that need would reach 3.5 billion by 2050. Behind those estimates are ordinary acts: hearing a teacher, navigating a building, or saying goodnight. [28]

An environment can exclude a person even when the barrier is avoidable. Stairs prevent a wheelchair user from entering a place a ramp would make accessible. A meeting without usable captions can exclude a deaf colleague. Instead of asking only what someone can do, we need to ask what the setting allows them to do.

Technology can widen exclusion, especially when it is designed around an imaginary "normal" user. It can also reveal how unnecessary some exclusions always were.

Speech-recognition systems trained mainly on conventional speech can struggle with voices altered by disability or illness. Projects developed with people who have nonstandard speech collected more representative samples and adapted recognition to individual patterns. In 2022, Google reported an average reduction of more than eighty percent in median word-error rates from Project Euphonia's adapted systems. That was a company-reported research result, not a claim that every user or product would improve by that amount.

Project Relate pursued personalized recognition for individual users. [29]

The improvement came from changing the listener: the data it had learned from and the speech patterns it could recognize. The speaker should not have to become somebody else to use the tool.

The same pattern appears in quieter moments. A live caption catches the announcement in a crowded airport. A screen reader turns a university's digital library into a place a blind student can enter without asking permission. Text-to-speech allows someone who cannot use a telephone conventionally to call the utility company without recruiting a relative. Navigation software describes an intersection. Translation helps a newly arrived parent understand a school notice that would otherwise remain a locked door.

Access is a separate question. A caption can misread a name. A system can perform unevenly across voices or settings. Cost, connectivity, and a design update can put a useful tool out of reach. WHO and UNICEF's 2022 report estimated that nearly one billion people lacked the assistive products they needed. WHO's fact sheet reported access as low as three percent in some low-income countries. An invention can exist while the person who needs it still cannot use it. [28]

A voice recovered

In a documented clinical study described by UC Davis in 2024, Casey Harrell, a man with ALS and severely impaired speech, used an investigational brain-computer interface to communicate. Implanted sensors recorded activity associated with attempted speech; machine-learning methods helped convert it into text and synthesized speech. Software used recordings of his earlier voice to shape the spoken output. The study concerned one participant using an experimental system, not a generally available cure. It demonstrated a route toward communication that mattered in his life. [30]

The achievement is not that a machine has acquired a human voice for its own sake. It is that a person has gained another way to enter the conversation. The distinction changes what we celebrate. Accuracy and speed matter because they serve expression. The goal is not an impressive system detached from its user, but a life with more room for that user's intention.

We should be careful with the word restored. A communication tool may restore an ability or expand a possibility. It does not restore a person's humanity, because that humanity was never absent. Language that turns access into a story of becoming fully human again can unintentionally repeat the exclusion it means to overcome.

Help and authorship

Many people rely on assistance to express themselves. A person may communicate through a device, a translator, a caregiver, signs, movement, or a pace unfamiliar to the listener. The listener's responsibility includes making enough room for the expression to arrive without assuming that difference means absence.

AI may be used to predict words, clarify speech, or support translation. Such help raises a question about authorship: whose intention does the output express? The answer should be grounded in the user's control, ability to correct, and informed preferences, not simply in how fluent the result sounds.

Imagine a system that helps a person compose a message slowly. A prediction can reduce effort. But if the system repeatedly supplies the most likely phrase, and other people accept it before the user can revise it, convenience may begin to displace intention. A humane design makes correction possible and treats the user's choice as authoritative, even when a different sentence would be faster.

The extra minute changes who gets to speak on their own terms. Assistance should not require someone to surrender what they mean. A tool can make expression easier while the people around it make expression harder by rushing or assuming.

The opposite error is to deny assistance in the name of purity. A listener might insist on an unassisted response as the only authentic one, ignoring that the tool is how the person can participate. Independence is not the absence of all support. It often means having appropriate control over the support on which we rely.

Who sets the pace

Conversation has rhythms. People interrupt, overlap, pause, and move on. These rhythms can feel natural to those they suit and exclusionary to those they do not. A person whose response takes longer may be present throughout the exchange and still find that the opportunity to contribute keeps closing before they can enter.

A daughter who waits while her father composes a sentence changes that rhythm. Her waiting is not a performance of virtue. It is part of making the conversation genuinely shared. The device can help produce words; the people at the table must leave room for the speaker.

This kind of accommodation need not make every interaction solemn. Humor, irritation, disagreement, and ordinary impatience remain part of life. The goal is not to turn a person into an inspirational object. It is to make the room large enough for the full person, including the parts that do not fit a sentimental story.

A society can invest in remarkable technology while failing at this ordinary hospitality. It can celebrate a device in a video and still organize meetings, classrooms, or services so that the people using it are routinely left behind. Access needs to be judged in lived participation, not only in available equipment.

A benefit that reaches the person

Research demonstrations deserve attention, but a successful demonstration is not the end of the access story. A person may need training, maintenance, reliable power, appropriate fitting, technical support, and a way to replace or repair equipment. Financial and institutional arrangements can determine whether a capability becomes part of a sustainable life.

These are general considerations, not claims about the availability or suitability of a particular experimental device. Their importance follows from the difference between making something possible and making it dependably usable. An exciting technology can remain beyond reach even after its technical potential is established.

People with disabilities should be participants in defining useful progress. What an observer finds impressive may not match the user's highest priority. A simpler, reliable feature can matter more than a dramatic demonstration. Privacy, comfort, portability, and control may outweigh a marginal improvement in performance.

That participation also changes the questions asked of AI. Instead of beginning with what a model can do, we can begin with what a person wants to be able to do, what currently prevents it, and which combination of technology and social change would help. Sometimes the answer will involve advanced AI. Sometimes it will involve a ramp, an accessible document, a patient listener, or an institution willing to alter a rule.

The lesson is not that simpler help is morally superior. It is that the person defines the purpose. Innovation becomes humane when the excitement of possibility remains connected to the user's actual life.

The human already there

When somebody regains a way to speak, the visible transformation can be extraordinary. But people should not have to produce such a transformation to deserve attention. The person for whom a device does not work, who cannot access it, or who chooses a different form of communication remains equally entitled to dignity and participation.

Staying human cannot mean protecting unaided performance. That would exclude many human lives. Speech, memory, productivity, and independence are not tests a person must pass to deserve belonging.

At the kitchen table, the man's tablet had finished speaking. His daughter set down two mugs. She had made his coffee out of habit before remembering that he could no longer drink it safely. For a second, both of them looked at the untouched cup.

Then he typed again.

"Still smells better than yours."

She laughed hard enough to cover her face. The untouched coffee remained between them.

CHAPTER 16

A Life Beyond Usefulness

The first person to speak in the recovery meeting had rehearsed the sentence in his car. He had led a company, raised children, and spent decades becoming the person others called in a crisis. The sentence felt more dangerous than any decision he had made at work.

“I need help.”

The people in the circle waited. One nodded. The man had to decide whether to say the next sentence.

The meeting could not do the next part for him. He had to decide whether to return and whether to use the help offered. Saying one honest sentence was a beginning, not evidence that the problem had been solved.

Vulnerability is not indiscriminate disclosure. Trust must be earned, power matters, and some environments punish honesty. The demand to “bring your whole self” can become another way institutions extract from people without protecting them. Courage includes knowing where truth is safe enough to become useful.

After the meeting, another man approached him in the parking lot. “Me too,” he said. They exchanged numbers.

The first man sat in his car with the new contact open, unsure whether he would use it. Asking once had not made asking easy.

When being useful has become part of our identity, receiving care can feel like losing our place. It may be easier to arrange help for someone else than let them arrange it for us. We need room for both roles. No one remains the capable one in every part of life.

What love refuses to optimize

Each morning, a man helped his wife button her shirt. Her hands had once moved quickly through a thousand ordinary tasks. Illness had slowed them. If he took over completely, they could be downstairs in minutes. Instead he waited while she tried the first buttons herself.

Love had become a negotiation with time. Some days she wanted help. Some days help felt like evidence of everything being lost. The husband learned that efficiency could be a form of theft when it removed the remaining act a person needed to call her own.

Some days the husband guessed wrong. He helped when she wanted time, or waited when she was already tired. Asking sounded less graceful than knowing. It worked better.

People lose sleep, rearrange futures, and spend years caring for bodies that will not recover. Those choices can be loving. They can also exhaust a caregiver who has too little help. Admiring the sacrifice is not enough; the person making it needs a life that can sustain it.

Artificial intelligence may help couples communicate, remember what matters, divide work, detect patterns, and find words during conflict. It may support caregivers who are overwhelmed and people whose loneliness has become dangerous. These are worthy uses.

A response matters partly because of the history behind it. "I am here" carries the mornings when leaving would have been easier, the promises kept badly and then repaired, the knowledge of what help this person can bear today. A tool can support that history. It cannot have lived it for us.

The husband eventually fastened the final button. His wife looked toward the mirror, adjusted the collar, and asked whether he was ready. The question retained the grammar of their earlier life, when she had always been the one waiting.

"I am," he said.

They went downstairs slowly. At the last step, she asked him to stop holding her arm. He let go and remained close.

Room for delight

A life made entirely of duty would miss something too. We need experiences that do not have to improve us, help someone, or justify the time they take. A ridiculous game, music played badly with friends, an afternoon looking at something beautiful: pleasure belongs here without a productivity argument.

Technology can be part of that pleasure. On December 24, 1968, Apollo 8 astronaut William Anders saw Earth rise beyond the moon's horizon. After a first photograph in black and white, he and his crewmates hurried to find color film.

The image that followed carried human improvisation inside technological achievement: a machine had taken them there, and a person noticed what deserved to be seen. [31]

The photograph became known as Earthrise. It did not reveal a planet nobody knew existed. It revealed the known world from a position no human eye had occupied. Distance changed meaning. Borders vanished. The place containing every human argument appeared fragile enough to hold in one gaze.

Understanding what we are seeing need not diminish the experience. Learning why the moon is visible in daylight can make a child look again. Learning how far its light has traveled can make an adult stay outside a little longer. Knowledge and wonder can keep each other company.

On a connected screen, extraordinary images can arrive in an endless stream. This can expand perception and flatten it. A nebula, disaster, dance, joke, and advertisement pass beneath the same thumb. The rare becomes content. Wonder cannot survive on novelty alone; novelty demands escalation.

Not everything worth noticing will be chosen for us. An unexpected conversation, a patch of weather, a piece of music someone else puts on: part of the pleasure is meeting something we would not have requested.

AI can help us make something playful, explore a subject, or imagine a world. Enjoy that help. Also leave some room to make a thing slowly, badly, or entirely by hand if the making is what you wanted. The finished object is not always the whole reason for the activity. You get to decide which part of the experience to keep.

The person after the title

In an illustrative scene, a retired worker visits the place where she spent most of her adult life. The entrance has changed. A younger employee offers to help her find the office she once knew without thinking. Her photograph is still on a wall, but the name of the department is different.

She is pleased that the work continues. She is also unsettled by how easily it continues without her. At home, people have told her to enjoy having time. She does enjoy parts of it. The difficult feeling is not simply boredom. It is uncertainty about where the usefulness that once organized her days has gone.

Long before AI, retirement could disturb a person's sense of worth. More capable machines sharpen an old question: if a role no longer needs us, what else do we know about who we are?

The answer cannot be that the person must immediately find a new way to be productive. Contribution matters, but rest, pleasure, relationship, and existence do not become legitimate only after a person demonstrates another useful output. A life is not a position that must be continually renewed through performance.

The wish to make something

AI-generated art and writing can provoke strong reactions partly because creation is not only a way to obtain an object. It is also a way to discover what we think, develop skill, and communicate that someone was here paying attention.

A generated image may delight a viewer. A person using assistance may make something they could not otherwise produce. Those possibilities need not be denied to protect the value of human creative practice. The harder question is how assistance affects the process and the range of work that enters a culture.

In a 2024 experiment, Anil Doshi and Oliver Hauser studied short-story writing with access to AI-generated ideas. Assisted stories received higher evaluations on measures of creativity and quality, particularly for some writers, while the collection of assisted stories became more similar. This was a bounded experiment in short fiction, not proof that AI inevitably improves every artist or makes all culture uniform. It reveals a tension worth examining between individual assistance and collective variety. [32]

The tension has an everyday form. A person asks for a stronger opening and receives a familiar rhythm that works. Many other people may receive versions of a similar rhythm. Each revision can feel like an improvement while the wider landscape becomes less surprising. This is a possibility to notice, not a reason to reject every suggestion.

Creative judgment includes deciding what to keep that is awkward, particular, or initially unpromising. A memory may matter because it does not fit the expected pattern. A voice may be worth hearing because it resists the most immediately polished version. Assistance is most useful when it expands the maker's choices rather than narrowing them to what already looks successful.

The crooked bowl

A child makes a bowl from clay. It leans to one side, and its opening is too narrow for the purpose the child originally intended. An adult could buy a better bowl for very little money. A machine might produce a design closer to the imagined result.

None of that explains why the child wants to keep it. The object records an encounter with a material, an intention revised, and a difficulty endured. Its value includes the making. To judge it only as a container would be to miss the experience through which it came into the child's life.

Adults need forms of making that are allowed to matter in this way too. Singing without an audience, repairing something imperfectly, writing a letter, cooking a meal, or learning an instrument can be worthwhile without producing the best available result. The abundance of superior output does not make participation obsolete.

This is especially important in a culture that invites people to compare their beginnings with polished work from everywhere. If the right to create depends on being exceptional, most people will become spectators. AI could intensify that pressure by making impressive output more common. It could also help people enter creative activity with less fear. The design and use of the help matter.

An adult helping the child might demonstrate how to support the wall of the bowl. They might provide a tool that makes shaping easier. They might also know when to stop correcting. The purpose is not only a better bowl. It is a child who remains willing to make things.

A dignity that does not fluctuate

It is easy to affirm human worth in general and still organize daily life around conditions that contradict it. We praise dignity, then become impatient with people who need more time. We say everyone matters, then treat a loss of earning power as a loss of social importance. We celebrate care, then make the people receiving it feel like burdens.

AI may change which performances are scarce or economically rewarded. That makes it especially important to distinguish value in a market from value as a person. The distinction is ethical; no productivity study can establish it for us. We either build institutions and relationships that honor it, or we leave it as a sentence we admire while living otherwise.

Equal dignity does not mean that every action is equally good or that responsibility disappears. People can cause harm and must answer for it. Skills can matter greatly in choosing who should perform a task. The point is that a person's basic claim to humane treatment does not rise and fall with their comparative efficiency.

For the retired worker, this might mean that belonging is not dependent on returning as a volunteer whenever the organization needs help. For a child, it means that affection is not conditional on achievement. For someone living with illness, it means that receiving care is not a debt that must be repaid through inspirational performance.

These are not abstract exceptions to ordinary life. Most lives move through dependence and capability, activity and rest, giving and receiving. A humane world makes room for that movement rather than treating one period of high output as the standard everyone should maintain forever.

The visit after the visit

The retired worker leaves the building and meets a friend for lunch. At first she describes the new entrance, the young employee, the changed department. She makes the story funny because the sadness feels disproportionate. Her friend laughs, then asks whether going back was harder than she expected.

For a moment, she does not need to be the experienced professional, the grateful retiree, or the person with a plan for the next chapter. She can simply admit that she misses being needed in a way she understood.

The conversation does not produce a new identity. It makes room for the unfinished one. Later she may choose work, service, study, rest, or some combination she has not yet imagined. None of those choices has to prove that her life remains worth having.

CHAPTER 17

The Things We Cannot Keep

The box had been on the top shelf for years. In this fictional scene, two siblings bring it down while sorting their mother's apartment. Inside are letters, photographs, a recipe written on the back of an envelope, and a small recorder with a damaged label. They disagree about what should be kept before they know what is on the tape.

When they finally hear it, the recording is not the important family occasion they expected. Their mother is explaining how to make something. Halfway through, somebody off microphone asks a question, and she becomes briefly irritated. A cupboard closes. There is a laugh, then several seconds of silence while she looks for a word.

One sibling begins to cry. The other turns the volume down, then apologizes because that was not what was needed. They listen again. The ordinary interruption is what makes the voice feel most familiar.

Later, one wonders whether the available recordings could be used to generate new speech in her voice. The idea brings comfort to one and unease to the other. They both miss the same person. They do not want the same thing from the traces she left.

A memory and a new statement

A recording preserves a particular expression from a particular time. A generated simulation can produce words the person never spoke. The difference is not merely technical. It changes the relationship between the material and the life it appears to represent.

Someone may find meaning in a clearly identified simulation. Another may feel that an imitation crosses a boundary. These reactions can coexist within a family. Neither should be dismissed simply because the technology is possible or because an observer believes there is one proper way to grieve.

The person represented matters too. Their wishes, if known, should not disappear because they are no longer available to object. Consent given for one use of a recording does not automatically settle every later use. The people affected may need to discuss what is being created, who can access it, and how it will be distinguished from genuine records.

Grief does not give every family the same answer. Consent, expectations, and the effect on the living all matter. A simulation should not be mistaken for the person, or treated as a substitute for care when someone needs help.

There is also a question of continuity. A service may change, disappear, or become inaccessible. A family considering an emotionally significant use deserves to understand those conditions. The warmth of a simulated voice should not hide the practical fragility of the system producing it.

The sentence they would never have said

The siblings try a simple demonstration with material they have permission to use. The result sounds recognizable enough to startle them. Then it says something polished about love that their mother would never have phrased that way. One laughs involuntarily. The other is upset by the laugh.

The disagreement reveals that resemblance is not identity. A voice can carry familiar acoustic features while the sentence belongs to a different process. The imitation may be moving, but it cannot establish that the represented person intended what it says.

They stop the demonstration. They have not reached a universal conclusion about the technology. They have discovered that this use requires more care than either expected. For now, they keep the original recording and make copies so it will not be lost to a failing device.

What forgetting is not

Preserving a memory can be an act of love. It can also become tangled with fear that letting a detail fade means betraying the person. Digital abundance may intensify that fear by making total preservation seem almost possible. If everything can be stored, what does it mean to let anything go?

Human remembering has never been a perfect archive. We recall some details vividly and lose others. A smell or a phrase returns unexpectedly. Stories change as different people tell them. None of this guarantees a faithful record, but the imperfection is not evidence that affection was inadequate.

Technology can help preserve material that would otherwise disappear. Digitizing a fragile recording, organizing photographs, or making a transcript accessible may be valuable. The purpose need not be to create a complete substitute for the person. It can be to make traces available for the living people who want to remember together.

AI may assist with organization or restoration, but alterations need to remain distinguishable from the original. An enhanced image can introduce details. A generated continuation can sound plausible without being historical. A family archive should not quietly become a mixture in which later inventions are mistaken for what actually happened.

The desire for a more vivid memory should not erase the difference between evidence and imagination. Both can have a place. Their meanings depend partly on knowing which is which.

The time no system can return

There are losses that information cannot reverse. A transcript can preserve words but cannot recreate the opportunity to ask a question while the speaker was alive. A photograph can reveal a detail but cannot restore the afternoon in which it was taken. A system may generate a response to an unsaid sentence without changing the history that made the sentence unsaid.

This limitation need not make the help worthless. People find comfort in letters never sent, conversations imagined, and rituals that acknowledge absence. The ethical issue is not that a generated exchange is automatically meaningless. It is whether its meaning is understood honestly.

The distinction also speaks to life before loss. We can become so occupied with preserving an experience that we barely inhabit it. We can collect material for future memory while leaving little room for the present relationship. The problem is not photography or recording. It is allowing preservation to replace participation.

A parent can put down a camera without losing the right to remember the moment. A child can hear a story without needing to record every word. A family can choose to preserve something carefully and still leave part of an evening unmeasured. There is no perfect balance that applies to every household. There is a choice worth noticing.

Death is not the only ending we struggle to accept. A child outgrows a version of childhood. A relationship changes. An ability is lost. Technology may preserve a record, but it cannot promise that life will remain as it was.

The stranger we used to be

Memory also concerns our own earlier selves. A digital record may preserve opinions, mistakes, images, and relationships long after a person has changed. Some records serve accountability. Others can make it difficult to outgrow an interpretation formed in a different period of life.

The ethical question is not solved by demanding either perfect forgetfulness or permanent exposure. People harmed by wrongdoing may need records. People trying to build a different life may need a fair chance to be understood in the present. Institutions must navigate these interests with attention to context, not a single reflex about what technology can store.

AI can make old material easier to search, combine, and summarize. That increases the importance of accuracy and context. A summary of a life can be efficient while being deeply misleading if it treats an old fragment as a complete account of the person now standing before us.

There is a relational version of the same problem. We can keep treating someone as the child, colleague, or partner they once were, even after they have changed. A machine did not invent that habit. Greater access to old material may reinforce it unless we remain willing to encounter the present person.

To be known should not mean being frozen. Human relationships need memory, but they also need opportunities for surprise, correction, and growth. A person deserves more than an indefinitely repeated summary of their least representative moment.

The ordinary recording

At the end of the afternoon, the siblings keep the recipe, the letters they recognize, and several photographs neither can fully explain. They set aside other things for relatives to consider. The box is not empty, but it is lighter.

Before leaving, they listen once more to the recording. This time they notice the question from the other room. It is about where a serving dish has gone. Their mother gives an answer, then changes her mind. The exchange leads them to a story neither had thought about in years, and they disagree over how it ended.

The disagreement becomes funny. One calls an aunt, who remembers a third version. For a while, the person they miss is present through the living relationships that continue to interpret and carry her memory. No one has to pretend that the phone call reverses the loss.

The siblings turn off the recording. One asks the other to stay for dinner. There is still work to do in the apartment, and more disagreements ahead. The invitation does not fix the grief. It gives the evening somewhere to go.

Repair

The argument

The argument began with a dishwasher and ended with the future of civilization.

Daniel believed Eli had loaded the machine carelessly. Eli believed Daniel had inspected the dishwasher because he was already angry about a missing assignment. Within three minutes they were no longer discussing plates. Daniel said Eli moved through the house as if other people were furniture. Eli said Daniel cared more about rules than reasons. Maya told them both to lower their voices, which made both voices louder.

Rosa left the room. Sofia remained because children often watch family conflict with the concentration adults reserve for weather alerts.

"You have no idea how easy you have it," Daniel said.

The sentence crossed the room and broke something. Eli's face changed.

"Right," he said. "Because if my life isn't as hard as yours, nothing can hurt."

He went upstairs. The door closed - not slammed, which somehow made the silence worse.

Daniel began unloading the dishwasher. Maya stood beside him.

"You were trying to teach responsibility," she said.

"Thank you."

"That wasn't the end of the sentence."

They waited. Marriage had taught them that the first available words were often the least useful.

"Go talk to him," she said.

"He doesn't want to talk."

"Neither do you."

Daniel found Eli sitting on the floor beside his bed. He began with an explanation, heard himself, and stopped.

"I was unfair," he said.

Eli looked up, suspicious. Apologies from parents can sound like doors with hidden alarms.

"I want you to help here," Daniel continued. "But I made your pain compete with mine. I'm sorry."

Eli did not deliver a speech. He nodded once. Then, after a while, he said the missing assignment was not missing. He had never started it. He could not make himself begin anything lately. Every task seemed to arrive carrying proof that he would fail it.

Daniel sat on the floor. The dishwasher remained open downstairs.

The apology did not finish the conversation. Daniel still expected Eli to contribute at home, and Eli still needed help with the assignment. They agreed to speak with the school counselor about how difficult beginning had become. The next week they argued again. But "That wasn't the end of the sentence" gave them a way to stop before the argument became the whole relationship.

Lucía's daughter

Three weeks after Rosa learned that Lucía had died, a message arrived from a woman named Elena. She was replying to a message Eli had left on the memorial page with Rosa's permission.

Rosa read the message repeatedly without answering. The dead preserve a relationship in its last known condition. Replying would allow time to move again.

Elena lived outside Sacramento. They spoke on a Sunday afternoon. At first they exchanged facts: dates, addresses, employers, the names of people neither had seen in decades. Then Elena asked what her mother had been like before becoming a mother.

The question opened a door.

Rosa described the laundromat in El Paso, the yellow dress, the notes beside the sink, the way Lucía sang badly and without embarrassment. She told Elena that her mother once spent half a week's pay on a bus ticket so Rosa would not face a medical appointment alone.

Elena was quiet.

"She never talked about Texas," she said.

Elena sent photographs. In one, Lucía was seventy, seated beneath a tree, laughing with the same refusal of self-consciousness Rosa remembered. Rosa placed the photograph beside the digital frame.

Rosa could not recover the years she had missed with Lucía. She could still choose what to do with the memory, and how honestly to speak about it with the people who remained.

Rosa began recording stories for Elena. Not polished histories. Three-minute voice messages about burnt beans, bus stations, first jobs, and a borrowed yellow dress.

PART 6

What Is Progress For

What would make a more powerful world a more humane one?

CHAPTER 18

Where the Saved Time Goes

The night shift

At 2:40 in the morning, Maya entered Room 814 carrying a cup of ice chips and found Mr. Bell staring at the ceiling.

His chart said seventy-eight, congestive heart failure, fall risk, fluid restriction. It did not say that he had repaired elevators for forty-one years, disliked pears, or had not slept without his wife beside him since 1969. She had died in the spring.

"Couldn't sleep?" Maya asked.

"I'm practicing," he said.

She understood what he meant and wished she did not.

The unit was short-staffed. A monitor sounded two rooms away, and a colleague went to check it. Maya had medications due soon, notes unfinished, and a bladder she had ignored since midnight. She looked toward the hall, then back at Mr. Bell.

She pulled the chair closer.

Mr. Bell told her about elevators. He said he had spent half his working life asking people to stop forcing the doors. Everybody wanted one more second, then complained that the machine was broken.

"That seems like more than elevator advice," Maya said.

"Mostly it's door advice," he said. "People never listen to that either."

Her next medication round was due. Maya stood.

"Go," he said. "I know I'm not the only one."

She returned twelve minutes later. He was asleep.

At breakfast, his daughter arrived carrying a blue sweater. Mr. Bell died that afternoon, while Maya was home trying to sleep through a neighbor's lawn mower. She learned about it when she returned for her next shift. The room had already been cleaned.

For days, Maya remembered the unfinished cup of ice chips. She had returned when she could, and it still felt insufficient. Caregivers need colleagues and staffing plans that can carry some of that weight. Praise for going beyond the job cannot become a way to make an impossible job acceptable.

Months later, an administrator presented a plan for automated documentation. Maya supported the possibility of spending less time writing notes. She also knew what would happen if the staffing plan treated every recovered minute as room for another patient.

"What will the saved minutes be for?" she asked.

The administrator said the hospital could not promise a longer visit for every patient. The budget and the waiting list were real. Maya asked whether the trial could at least measure time at the bedside as carefully as time spent documenting.

They added it to the evaluation. No extra nurse arrived on the next shift. Maya still had to leave some conversations unfinished. But the promise of returned time now had a measure that could contradict it.

Where the saved hours went

Eleanor W. Dillon and colleagues studied access to an integrated generative AI tool among 7,137 knowledge workers across 66 firms. Their November 2025 working-paper revision reports that, in the second half of the six-month experiment, the users among those given access spent about two fewer hours on email each week and less time working outside regular hours. The researchers did not detect broader changes in the quantity or composition of tasks from individual access alone. [33]

The finding leaves a personal question as well as an organizational one. When a task becomes easier, do we use any of the gain to learn something, rest, or reconnect? Or do we allow a new volume of work to arrive before making that choice? [33]

The time that disappeared

Imagine a person finishing an administrative task in fifteen minutes that once took an hour. Forty-five minutes have been freed. The person is relieved. By the end of the week, however, the calendar contains four additional requests, and the day ends at the usual time.

The forty-five minutes have not vanished mysteriously. They have been claimed. A manager, a customer, a household, or the person themselves has found another use for it. The question is whether that use reflects a deliberate priority or simply the tendency of available capacity to become expected capacity.

Efficiency can be valuable even when it does not create leisure. A public service may reduce a waiting list. A small organization may survive. A worker may avoid unpaid work after hours. These are meaningful gains. The mistake is promising more time for life without examining the decisions that determine where the time goes.

The word saved can imply that the resource is now safely ours. In practice, time often requires protection after it has been recovered. A system can make a task faster while leaving unchanged the incentives that fill every opening. The result is acceleration without relief.

Care has more than one clock

Some parts of care are rightly judged by speed. An urgent need should be recognized quickly. A result should not be delayed unnecessarily. A person should not spend hours navigating a process that could be made clear in minutes.

Other parts require a different kind of time. A frightened patient may need an explanation repeated. A caregiver may need room to ask a question they are embarrassed to raise. A child may only reveal the real concern after several apparently unrelated sentences. Making those exchanges faster is not always the same as making them better.

An institution must balance these demands. It cannot promise unlimited time to every person. It can, however, recognize that the important work sometimes appears inefficient when measured too narrowly. An extra conversation may reveal information that changes the next step. A pause may prevent a misunderstanding. The value may not be visible in the simplest record of throughput.

AI can support the balance by reducing some burdens and making information easier to use. It can also distort the balance if every improvement is converted into a new target that removes the time needed to exercise judgment. The ethical question lives in the deployment, not only in the technology.

The people doing the work should have a voice in deciding which burdens are most worth reducing. A feature that impresses a purchaser may not address the problem that consumes a practitioner's day. Listening to that difference is part of making efficiency real rather than ceremonial.

Rest without a justification

There is another possibility for saved time: nothing visibly productive happens in it. A person rests. They sit outside, talk with a friend, take a nap, or do not immediately decide what to do next. In an output-centered account, this may appear to be a missed opportunity.

But the purpose of human life cannot be an indefinitely increasing rate of production. Rest can be necessary, pleasurable, and worthwhile without being defended only as a method for returning to work more efficiently. A person is not a battery whose downtime matters solely because it improves later performance.

This does not deny obligations. People depend on one another, and necessary work remains. It asks that the distribution of time include a meaningful claim for the people whose lives are being made more efficient. If the benefit of a tool never reaches their experience of living, we should be cautious about describing it as liberation.

People also need different kinds of rest. Solitude may restore one person and deepen another's isolation. An activity may feel restful to someone whose day is sedentary and exhausting to someone whose work is physical. A humane account does not turn one preferred lifestyle into the standard everybody must adopt.

The technology could help people discover or arrange what they need. It should not convert rest into another monitored achievement. A walk need not become valuable only after it is tracked. A conversation need not produce an insight. An evening can be good without evidence suitable for a report.

The person who does not receive the dividend

Some people will experience AI mainly as an increase in expectations. Their work may be evaluated against faster output, while the time needed for supervision, correction, and learning remains invisible. A household may gain new administrative responsibilities because a service assumes everyone can now manage them digitally.

These are possible patterns to examine, not outcomes that can be assumed in every setting. The point is that a technical saving in one part of a process can move effort to another person. A provider may become more efficient while a user spends longer resolving confusing automated responses. An employer may reduce one task while increasing the burden of checking several systems.

The relevant measure is therefore the whole experience, including errors and the work of recovery. An arrangement that appears fast only when everything goes well may be slow and distressing when something goes wrong. The people handling the exceptions deserve to be included in the account.

This also requires attention to unpaid time. A family member helping an older relative use a new service may be doing labor the service no longer provides. Their willingness is valuable, but it should not be treated as an inexhaustible resource. A humane design asks whether support has genuinely improved or merely been transferred out of sight.

A different ending to the day

Return to the imagined worker whose administrative task became faster. The organization decides to evaluate the change over time, including quality, correction work, and employee experience. It discovers that some saved time is real and some was overstated. The revised arrangement leaves a modest, dependable reduction in late work.

The improvement is less spectacular than the original demonstration. It is also more meaningful. A parent can reach an evening activity without apologizing for being late. Another worker can attend an appointment without inventing an excuse. Someone simply arrives home with less of the day still clinging to them.

The result need not be dramatic to matter. A little relief, repeated across ordinary days, changes what a person has left to give.

Maya's saved time might become a conversation at a bedside. On another day, it might become an earlier trip home. Both can be humane. Caring for others does not require the caregiver to disappear from the calculation of whose life matters.

CHAPTER 19

A Home That Remembers Its Purpose

The family's phones slept in a wooden box near the door. The box was not elegant. One corner had split, and the youngest child had written a name on the lid. Its importance came from what happened after the devices entered it.

At first, dinner became worse. Everyone felt the missing escape. Complaints lasted longer. The children argued. The parents discovered how often a glance at a screen had allowed them to leave discomfort without resolving it. One evening a parent had to keep a phone nearby for an expected work call. A child asked why the rule only counted for some people.

The adults could have answered with authority. Instead they explained the call, set the phone where everyone could see it, and agreed to leave the table if it rang. The exception had a reason and an end. It did not become permission to check everything else.

Over time, conversation became ordinary: a story about school, a joke repeated badly, a silence nobody rushed to fill.

Some dinners were still unpleasant. The box prevented one kind of departure. It could not make the people around the table listen.

A human home is not a home without technology. It is a place where technology knows its role. Tools should reduce burdens, widen access, create safety, and connect the people who cannot be present. They should not become the emotional climate.

A boundary is easier to keep when the room helps. A charging place outside the bedroom removes one decision at bedtime. A separate alarm clock lets the phone stay elsewhere. A table can have room for a person's communication device without becoming a place where everybody scrolls.

The arrangement should fit the people living with it. An on-call worker may need one notification channel open. A teenager may need privacy to speak with a friend. A parent whose children live elsewhere may need the screen to bring the family to dinner. The point is to know which use serves the relationship and which use interrupts it.

AI needs agreements too. A family might welcome help planning meals while keeping private conversations out of the tool. A child might use an explanation for learning while following the school's rules about submitted work. An adult might want help understanding a disagreement while declining to have their messages copied into a service. These uses should be discussed with the people affected, not silently treated as permissions that come with the device.

Do not make an AI response the deciding vote in a family argument. It has received the account somebody chose to provide. Use it to find a question you have missed, then ask the person who is actually there.

Some households cannot protect a daily dinner. Shift work, multiple jobs, caregiving, and unstable schedules make that promise unrealistic. A ten-minute breakfast, a weekly walk, or a call on the bus may be the time available. It deserves protection too. Presence should not become another standard by which an exhausted family is told it has failed.

Adults need to keep the agreement visible in their own behavior. When they break it, repair can be plain: I was checking something while you were talking. I missed what you said. Would you tell me again? Then the device has to move. A confession repeated without a change becomes another interruption.

The home also needs room to be enjoyable. A shared game can include a screen. A quiet evening can mean separate activities in the same room. Nobody should have to turn every dinner into a meaningful conversation to prove the arrangement is working.

No single shape of home

Homes do not all contain the same people or follow the same rules. Some are shared by partners, friends, several generations, or people living alone. A useful agreement begins with the lives actually being lived there.

For a person living alone, a useful AI tool may make an evening less difficult or help organize essential tasks. The humane question is not whether this resembles a traditional household. It is whether the tool supports the person's purposes and leaves them with appropriate control, accurate information, and connections they value.

For a crowded household, the challenge may be finding privacy rather than increasing contact. A device that listens or records can affect people who did not choose to install it. The convenience of one resident does not erase the interests of others sharing the space.

The agreement beneath the device

An imagined group of housemates begins using a shared assistant for shopping and schedules. At first, the arrangement is useful. Then one person discovers that a private appointment appears in a shared summary. Nobody intended harm. They had not discussed what the system could access or what should remain separate.

Their first argument concerns who changed the setting. The more important conversation concerns what each person reasonably expected. A technical permission may have been granted by one account holder without meaningful agreement from everyone affected. The household needs a social agreement as well as a configuration.

This does not require treating every convenience as a crisis. It requires recognizing that shared spaces contain overlapping rights and preferences. A person may welcome reminders and object to recording. Another may need accessibility features that others find unfamiliar. The solution should emerge from the actual people and needs, not from the assumption that the default is neutral.

The housemates change the arrangement. They separate some accounts, stop sharing certain information, and agree to discuss new features that affect the group. They also leave room to revise the agreement when circumstances change. The technology becomes easier to live with because its role becomes more explicit.

Help without a new kind of supervision

Families sometimes adopt technology to protect someone they love. A reminder may support medication routines. A location feature may reduce worry. A communication tool may make it easier to ask for help. Such uses can be valuable, but protection and control are not the same thing.

An adult who needs support still has preferences about privacy and independence. A child needs protection that changes as their capacity develops. A household should not treat affection as blanket permission to monitor whatever is technically available. The purpose, extent, and conditions of observation deserve discussion appropriate to the person's situation.

When safety, capacity, and competing responsibilities are difficult to resolve, professional guidance or a formal decision process may be needed. The person affected must still remain visible. Convenience for others is not automatically that person's best interest.

Rosa's changing needs create real concerns. The family must help without reducing her to a list of risks. A route, a reminder, or a calendar can be useful. So can asking what she wants to keep doing and what kind of assistance she would welcome.

The difference matters because independence is often relational. People remain able to choose and participate through support from others. The goal is not to prove that they need nobody. It is to ensure that needing help does not become a reason to stop asking them.

The home that can make a mistake

No household will handle technology perfectly. Someone will misunderstand a setting, become absorbed at the wrong moment, send a message they regret, or impose a rule they do not follow consistently. The quality of the home depends partly on what happens afterward.

A household that treats every error as a character verdict can make people conceal problems. A child may hide an unsettling interaction because they fear losing access or being blamed. An adult may avoid admitting they believed a false claim. The desire to appear competent can prevent the conversation through which competence develops.

Repair requires an environment in which a mistake can be described without every admission becoming a punishment. This is not the same as removing consequences. It means matching the response to what happened and preserving a route back to honesty.

In one imagined evening, Daniel realizes that a generated message he sent promised more help than he can actually provide. He could blame the tool or quietly hope nobody relies on the promise. Instead, he calls the person, explains the mistake, and makes a smaller commitment he can keep. The correction is embarrassing. It is also the part that makes the assistance compatible with trust.

Sofia overhears enough to ask why he did not just change the message. He explains that the other person may already have made plans. She is learning something about digital communication that no warning about screen time would teach as clearly: words can create obligations in another person's day.

A place where the person arrives first

What matters is whether the people in the room can express needs, set boundaries, receive help, and participate in decisions that affect them. Technology should support these possibilities. When it interferes, the arrangement should be open to change.

That principle travels beyond private households. A care residence, shelter, hospital ward, or communal living space also contains people whose routines can be shaped by systems they did not choose. The greater the institution's power, the more important it is to preserve privacy, explanation, and meaningful participation.

The Rivera family does not solve these questions once. They return to them as their circumstances change. Their humanity is not demonstrated by achieving a perfect rule. It is expressed in the willingness to notice when an arrangement is no longer serving someone and to respond without treating that person as the problem.

A good home, in whatever form it takes, should allow a human being to be more than the most convenient version of themselves. Our tools should help make that room possible.

CHAPTER 20

A World We Can Answer For

Before a flood reaches a home, there can be a period in which information changes what is possible. People may have time to move, protect important belongings, organize transport, or check on someone who cannot leave unaided. A useful warning is not merely a prediction of water. It is a chance for action before the options narrow.

Research by Grey Nearing and colleagues reported that an AI model could predict extreme river flooding in ungauged watersheds at lead times of up to five days with reliability comparable to, or better than, same-day forecasts from the comparison system. The work was incorporated into publicly available forecasts across more than eighty countries. These findings concern forecasting performance, not a demonstrated count of lives saved or a guarantee for every location and event. [34]

The example offers a different way to think about intelligence. The achievement is not only a machine displaying an impressive capability. It is the possibility that people may gain time to protect life. The value still depends on everything between the forecast and the person who needs to act.

The last distance

Imagine two households receiving the same warning. One has transport, a safe place to go, and enough flexibility to leave work. The other has an older relative who needs assistance, an employer who has not suspended the shift, and no clear account of how to reach the shelter.

The forecast may be equally accurate for both. The opportunity it creates is not equally usable. Information becomes protection through resources, trust, accessible communication, and a plan people can actually carry out. These conditions are part of the human system in which the technical system operates.

Who receives the warning? In which languages and formats? How does a person know it is genuine? What should they do if they cannot follow the suggested action? Who checks whether the people at greatest risk have been reached? These are operational questions with moral significance because their answers determine whose life the information can help protect.

A service designed around the easiest-to-reach user can produce an impressive average while missing those whose circumstances make help most urgent. That is a reason to examine the distribution of benefit, not to reject the technology. Better prediction and better human arrangements can strengthen one another.

The future as a public choice

Many descriptions of AI present the future as something moving toward us with an independent will. We are told to prepare, keep up, or avoid being left behind. There are real changes to understand. But the language of inevitability can hide decisions being made by people with particular interests and powers.

Which services adopt AI, how they evaluate it, what data they use, what alternatives remain, and how mistakes are corrected are choices. Not every individual has equal influence over them. That makes public accountability more important, not less.

A democratic conversation about technology does not require every citizen to understand model architecture. It requires understandable accounts of purpose, consequences, evidence, and responsibility. People can ask what a system is supposed to improve, who may be harmed, how its performance is being assessed, and what would lead to changing or stopping it.

The answers will sometimes be uncertain. A pilot may be necessary to learn what works. A trial can be responsible if its boundaries, risks, safeguards, and evaluation are appropriate. Experimentation becomes harder to defend when affected people cannot discover that they are part of it or cannot obtain help when it fails.

Communities will make different decisions. People who live with the consequences should have a way to question those decisions, describe what is happening, and help change what does not work.

A service that remains answerable

Consider an imagined public library introducing an AI-assisted service to help residents find information. The system can summarize material, support translation, and help someone formulate a question. Librarians remain available, and the service explains that generated answers may need checking.

The first months reveal unexpected uses. Some residents want help understanding ordinary correspondence. Others want to learn. A few bring sensitive questions that require privacy and professional referral rather than a confident automated response. The library adapts its procedures, learns from errors, and clarifies what the service can and cannot do.

The value lies partly in the technology and partly in the institution's willingness to remain responsible. A person can ask for help without having to accept a generated answer as the final word. The service connects them to resources and people rather than enclosing them inside an interface.

Now imagine a different version. The same technology is used primarily to reduce staffing. The remaining workers have little time to check outputs. Users are directed back to the system when they question an answer. On paper, the service handles more requests. In practice, some people are receiving less accountable help.

Counting completed interactions would miss the difference between these two services. One has moved a queue off the premises. The other has helped people get what they came for.

The right to stop

A society that wants beneficial innovation needs ways to discontinue uses that do not work. Stopping a deployment should not always be treated as humiliation or hostility to progress. Sometimes it is the result of taking evidence seriously.

This requires defining success before enthusiasm becomes the only standard. If a tool is meant to improve access, its evaluation should include people whose access was previously difficult. If it is meant to reduce workload, it should include the work of correction and oversight. If it is meant to improve a decision, it should be compared with a meaningful alternative rather than with an imaginary world containing no help at all.

The criteria may change as new information arrives, but changes should be explained. Otherwise, a project can protect itself by continually redefining the benefit it was supposed to deliver. Accountability includes the possibility that the original promise was not fulfilled.

Reversibility matters too. An organization should understand what happens if the service becomes unavailable, changes terms, or no longer meets its needs. A community should not discover that it has lost essential capacity only after it has become unable to operate without a single provider.

These concerns do not imply that institutions should avoid dependence altogether. Modern life depends on complex systems. They imply that essential dependence should be understood and managed, with contingency plans proportionate to the consequences of failure.

The people who get to object

Public discussion often favors those with time, confidence, expertise, or a recognized position. A consultation can be formally open while remaining difficult for people working irregular hours, using another language, caring for someone, or needing accessible formats.

Meaningful participation requires attention to those barriers. The people most affected may need practical support to contribute. A community meeting at an inconvenient time is not enough to establish that everyone had a fair chance to be heard. Nor should lack of attendance be interpreted automatically as agreement.

AI may help here by translating material, making documents easier to navigate, and supporting different forms of communication. It should not be used to generate the appearance of consent or to treat a summarized public response as a substitute for deliberation. The technology can carry voices; the institution still decides whether those voices can change anything.

Disagreement will remain. People may reasonably assign different weights to privacy, speed, cost, accuracy, autonomy, and access. A humane process makes the tradeoffs understandable and identifies who is responsible for the final choice. It does not promise to remove politics from decisions about how people live together.

More than damage control

An ethical conversation limited to preventing harm can become too small. Avoiding harm matters, but people also need a positive account of what the technology could help them do. Otherwise, the most ambitious visions are left to those selling capability, while everyone else is assigned the role of asking for restraints.

A more humane future could include easier access to knowledge, better support for communication, reduced burdens in care, and tools that help communities anticipate dangers. It could make participation possible for people previously excluded by cost, language, geography, or inaccessible design. These are possibilities to pursue with evidence, not outcomes to assume because the phrase AI appears in a proposal.

The positive vision should also include room for life that does not require a technological solution. A safe public space, a trusted institution, a dependable relationship, or a reasonable working schedule may address a problem more directly than a new interface. Progress can involve sophisticated tools and ordinary social commitments at the same time.

The forecast and the door

Return to the households receiving the warning. In a better version of the imagined arrangement, the message is understandable and trusted. Transport is available for people who need it. A local organization knows which residents have asked for assistance. Someone checks that a neighbor has received the information and can act.

The technical work and the human work have different forms. One identifies a risk across a large area. The other encounters particular lives within that area. Neither should be used as an excuse to neglect the other.

A person arrives at a door. Inside, an older resident has heard the warning but has not left because they do not know what will happen to a pet. The obstacle is small compared with the scale of the forecast and decisive in the resident's actual decision. A conversation finds an arrangement. The resident leaves.

This is a future worth building: powerful tools, people able to question and improve them, and a clear memory of whom they are meant to serve.

Return

Rosa's map

Rosa stopped driving after she turned onto the freeway in the wrong direction. No one was hurt. She corrected quickly and told no one for two weeks.

Losing the car meant losing more than transportation. It meant asking for groceries, appointments, church, the cemetery, the pharmacy. Dependence rearranged the geometry of her dignity.

The family created a shared calendar. Daniel ordered rides. Eli showed her how to track the car on a map. The system worked beautifully, except when it did not: a driver canceled, a location pin moved, an appointment ran late, a phone battery died.

One afternoon Rosa returned from the clinic furious. The driver had spoken to her slowly after hearing her accent. He asked whether someone managed her money. She gave him one star and then worried she had harmed his livelihood.

"Maybe he was trying to help," she said.

"Maybe," Maya answered. "And maybe help without respect is another kind of control."

They found a community transportation program staffed partly by retirees. The rides took longer. The cars were less polished. A driver named Warren learned that Rosa preferred the scenic road and disliked questions about grandchildren until she had volunteered information herself.

After the ride, Warren asked whether he had taken the right road. Rosa told him the other turn would have been better. He asked her to show him next time.

What remained on the table

The Rivera family did not become a model household.

Eli still slept beside his phone some nights. Daniel sometimes answered work messages during dinner. Maya missed two Sunday breakfasts in a row. Sofia discovered short-form videos and became remarkably hard to interrupt when asked to stop. Rosa forwarded an alarming article about bananas that had been disproved years earlier.

They learned to notice the moment a conversation thinned because everyone had left it without moving. They learned that "one second" rarely meant one second. They learned to ask whether a problem required information, help, witness, or simply company.

On Rosa's seventy-fourth birthday, the digital frame displayed the photograph of Rosa in the yellow dress, Lucía beside her. Elena joined by video from California. She held up a second photograph no one had seen: Lucía and Rosa sitting on the curb behind the laundromat, sharing an orange.

"Who took that?" Rosa asked.

No one knew.

After the call, the family remained at the table. Plates were empty. Thin blue smoke rose from the extinguished candles. Nothing prevented them from leaving.

Eli asked Rosa to tell the story again.

She began differently this time. Eli stayed to hear the difference.

CHAPTER 21

The Choices We Keep

A person sits with a draft of an apology. The assistant has made it clearer, calmer, and easier to read. It has also added a sentence promising that the mistake will never happen again. The person pauses. They want forgiveness. They are not sure they can make that promise.

Deleting the sentence may make the apology less impressive. It can make it more honest. The important choice happens before the message is sent: what am I willing to mean, do, and answer for?

That is a useful boundary for assistance. We can delegate parts of a task while keeping ownership of the purpose, the claims we pass on, and the commitments we make. Help with language does not settle the truth of a statement. Help comparing options does not decide whose needs count. Help with a relationship does not give us the other person's consent.

There is no single list of acts everyone must perform without AI. A person who relies on a communication device may need assistance with words of love, grief, and apology. The amount of help is not a measure of sincerity. Whether the person understands and stands behind the communication matters more than whether they produced every word unaided.

The same principle limits what we ask a tool to do to others. Their private information, voice, likeness, and memories are not just material for our purposes. Ask permission. Consider what the use will mean to them. A simulation can be technically impressive and still violate the relationship it claims to honor.

We also keep the duty to respond after acting. If a message hurts someone, hear what happened. If a fact is wrong, correct it. If a recommendation fails, revisit the assumptions. Assistance should make room for that work, not give us a way to disappear from it.

Remaining human alongside AI will require different choices in different lives. The question to carry forward is whether the way you use it leaves you more able to participate: to think, notice, make, care, question, and take responsibility. A tool can help you do those things. Keep a place for yourself in the doing.

A choice larger than a preference

The questions in this book can seem overwhelming when collected together. They concern classrooms, workplaces, public services, relationships, language, resources, and the changing capabilities of machines. No individual can personally supervise all of them. A demand to do so would turn responsibility into a form of exhaustion.

But responsibility is not identical to total control. A person can participate where they have knowledge, influence, or an obligation, while recognizing the limits of their position. Institutions and people with greater power carry greater responsibilities. The task is shared, not evenly distributed.

Some choices are intimate: whether to send words we mean, how to use help in a relationship, when to admit that we do not understand. Others are collective: what schools adopt, what employers expect, how public services remain accountable, and who receives the benefits of greater capacity. The first cannot substitute for the second. The second does not make the first irrelevant.

Courage without certainty

There will be moments when using AI is the responsible choice. It may help someone communicate, reduce an avoidable burden, or reveal a pattern relevant to safety. There will be other moments when limiting or declining its use is responsible. The evidence may be inadequate, the purpose inappropriate, or the risks unfairly imposed.

We will not always know in advance which choice will prove best. That uncertainty does not excuse indifference. It calls for proportionate caution, honest evaluation, and a willingness to change course. Courage can include trying a promising tool carefully. It can also include questioning a popular use before the problems are easy to see.

We should demand the same flexibility of institutions. A decision made under one set of conditions may need revision. Evidence should be allowed to change a policy. The people affected should be able to describe what the policy has become in practice, not only what it was intended to do.

The world we practice

The future is shaped partly by spectacular decisions and partly by repeated ordinary ones. What we reward becomes easier to repeat. What we make costly becomes harder to sustain. A workplace that rewards honesty about errors helps build one kind of relationship with technology. A workplace that rewards appearances while punishing correction helps build another.

A school that values explanation as well as output gives students a reason to remain involved in their learning. A service that makes appeals meaningful tells people they have not been reduced to a result. A household that can discuss a mistake without humiliation makes truth more likely to arrive while something can still be done.

These are not minor matters simply because they are ordinary. They form the environments in which people learn what is expected and what is possible. AI will enter those environments and change some of their capacities. It will not remove the human choices through which they acquire a character.

We learn a way of living by repeating it together. We practice impatience when every delay is treated as failure. We practice attention when an important concern is given room. We practice fairness when a person can question a decision without being punished for asking.

There will be failures. A humane world is not one in which nobody makes a mistake. It is one in which mistakes can be noticed, people can be heard, and repair remains possible.

The aim is not a flawless performance of humanity. It is a durable commitment to one another's reality.

A world worth entering

The argument of HUMAN is not that machines must remain weak for people to matter. It is that human worth must remain secure as machines become stronger. We should welcome capabilities that help people flourish while resisting arrangements that treat people as expendable obstacles to a more efficient system.

Imagine the reach of that standard. A child receives help that strengthens learning rather than merely improving a submission. A person with a communication disability is heard on their own terms. A worker gains capacity without losing a voice in the work. A community receives an early warning and the means to act on it. A family uses technology to cross distance and still undertakes the effort of relationship.

These are not guarantees or a complete description of the future. They are purposes against which actual choices can be judged. They give progress a human direction without pretending every disagreement has been settled.

There are more than eight billion lives behind the word humanity. Most will never become examples in a book or subjects in a research paper. They still contain fears, attachments, skills, disappointments, humor, and hopes that matter to the people living them. A powerful technology should widen our ability to recognize and serve those lives, not make their particularity seem inconvenient.

We cannot know every person. We can refuse to build a world whose success depends on forgetting that they are there.

Before You Go

On another Tuesday, Maya came home late enough that dinner was already being cleared. Daniel had saved her a plate. An AI meal planner had helped him use what remained in the fridge. Sofia had renamed the result "almost lasagna." She was at the table with a notebook, drawing something she kept covering with her hand.

Maya asked about it while looking at a message from work.

"Nothing," Sofia said.

Maya finished reading. Then she noticed that the notebook had closed.

"I asked and didn't listen," she said. "I'm sorry."

She put the phone on the counter and sat down. Sofia kept the notebook shut for a moment. Maya waited.

"You have to guess what it is."

Maya guessed a horse. It was a map. This was apparently a serious error. Sofia turned the notebook around and began explaining where the roads went.

There was a school beside a lake, which raised questions about flooding. Sofia moved the lake. The hospital had a garden on its roof. Rosa's house stood near a bus stop and a shop where the owner always had the right bread. Eli objected that the road leading to his friend's house ended in a field.

"You can walk the last part," Sofia said.

Daniel brought the plate. He asked whether the map needed a computer somewhere. Sofia pointed to several buildings. Of course there were computers. She had not thought it necessary to draw all of them.

Maya looked at the road stopping at the edge of the page.

"Where does this go?"

"I haven't done that part yet."

There was room on the other side. Maya moved her plate so Sofia could turn the notebook over.

It was a child's drawing, not a blueprint. The roads ignored distance, the buildings ignored cost, and nobody had yet worked out how the buses would turn around.

Yet Sofia had begun with something the adults were capable of forgetting. She had placed people and the things they needed to live. The tools belonged within that purpose. They were important without becoming the reason for the map.

Outside the kitchen, the world remained complicated. Maya's work problem still needed an answer. Daniel would return to decisions he could not make fair merely by caring about them. Eli would have to learn things that did not become his simply because an explanation was available. Rosa would need help and sometimes resent needing it. Their affection did not exempt them from any of this.

Sofia drew another road. She asked whether it should turn toward the lake or the school. Three people answered at once. She told them to wait.

There was laughter, an argument about the bus stop, and a complaint that dinner was getting cold. The page grew crowded. Someone found another sheet of paper.

The future was not theirs alone to draw. It would be shaped by people they knew and people they would never meet, by institutions, inventions, conflicts, and decisions beyond that room. But the lives at the table were among the lives it was supposed to serve.

That is where the question returns. Not only what can our machines become, but what kind of world will their growing power help us make? Who will be able to enter it? Who will be heard? What will we do with the time, knowledge, and possibilities we gain?

There will be more answers than we can use. There will still be people waiting to be understood.

Sofia handed Maya the pencil.

Acknowledgments

This book was built from the work of researchers, historians, clinicians, teachers, caregivers, technologists, workers, parents, and ordinary people who have tried to understand what helps human beings remain present to one another.

I am grateful to the people whose work is named in the notes, and to readers willing to question the argument as well as recognize themselves in it. The choices described here deserve that care.

Notes and Sources

Sources are numbered in the order they first appear. They document the reported events and research findings, not every ethical judgment drawn from them. The Rivera family and other unnamed scenes are illustrative fiction. Study dates and limits are retained so that a result from one setting is not mistaken for a universal rule.

1. Deep Blue and Garry Kasparov. IBM, "Deep Blue," including the 1996 and 1997 match history, system architecture, match score, and performance figures, https://www.ibm.com/history/deep-blue.

2. AlphaGo and Lee Sedol. Google DeepMind, "AlphaGo," match history and technical legacy, https://deepmind.google/research/alphago/. The official account identifies Lee as an eighteen-time world-title winner, reports the 4-1 result, and describes Moves 37 and 78 as exceptionally unlikely.

3. Generative AI risks. National Institute of Standards and Technology, Artificial Intelligence Risk Management Framework: Generative Artificial Intelligence Profile, NIST AI 600-1 (July 2024), https://doi.org/10.6028/NIST.AI.600-1. The profile identifies risks including false output, data privacy, and over-reliance. Everyday examples and proposed reader practices in this book are illustrative, not product certifications.

4. Tool-using AI systems. Erik Schluntz and Barry Zhang, "Building effective agents," Anthropic, December 19, 2024, https://www.anthropic.com/engineering/building-effective-agents. This developer account explains tool use, workflows, agent-directed steps, and the need for limits and human oversight. It is used to explain a system design, not to endorse a product or predict future capabilities.

5. Erik Brynjolfsson, Danielle Li, and Lindsey Raymond, "Generative AI at Work," The Quarterly Journal of Economics 140, no. 2 (2025): 889-942. https://doi.org/10.1093/qje/qjae044. The published study reports 5,172 customer-support agents and a 15 percent average productivity increase.

Figures refer to the published study rather than its earlier working-paper version.

6. Humanlike empathy in written answers. John W. Ayers and colleagues, "Comparing Physician and Artificial Intelligence Chatbot Responses to Patient Questions Posted to a Public Social Media Forum," JAMA Internal Medicine 183, no. 6 (2023): 589-596.
https://jamanetwork.com/journals/jamainternalmedicine/fullarticle/2804309.
The study compared answers to 195 forum questions; healthcare professionals evaluated anonymized responses. The 78.6 percent figure concerns preference across evaluations. It is not a patient-outcome measure or evidence that a system feels empathy. Response length differed between conditions.

7. Generative AI and work. International Labour Organization, "Generative AI and Jobs: A Global Analysis of Potential Effects on Job Quantity and Quality," Working Paper 96 (2023), and related policy brief,
https://www.ilo.org/resource/news/generative-ai-likely-augment-rather-destroy-jobs.

8. Shakked Noy and Whitney Zhang, "Experimental Evidence on the Productivity Effects of Generative Artificial Intelligence," Science 381 (2023): 187-192. https://doi.org/10.1126/science.adh2586. An experiment on specified professional writing tasks, not all occupations or long-term learning.

9. Michelle Vaccaro, Abdullah Almaatouq, and Thomas Malone, "When Combinations of Humans and AI Are Useful: A Systematic Review and Meta-analysis," Nature Human Behaviour 8 (2024): 2293-2303. https://doi.org/10.1038/s41562-024-02024-1. Covers 106 experimental studies; average results do not determine the outcome of a particular human-AI arrangement.

10. Teacher-supported AI tutoring in Nigeria. Martín E. De Simone and colleagues, "From Chalkboards to Chatbots: Transforming Learning in Nigeria, One Prompt at a Time," World Bank, January 9, 2025.
https://blogs.worldbank.org/en/education/From-chalkboards-to-chatbots-Transforming-learning-in-Nigeria.
See also World Bank Policy Research Working Paper 11125, "From Chalkboards to Chatbots: Evaluating the Impact of Generative AI on Learning Outcomes in Nigeria" (2025).

https://documents1.worldbank.org/curated/en/099548105192529324/pdf/IDU-c09f40d8-9ff8-42dc-b315-591157499be7.pdf.
The effect refers to a six-week, teacher-supported intervention and measured outcomes in its study setting, not a claim that six weeks of AI replaces years of schooling.

11. Assistance and independent learning. Hamsa Bastani and colleagues, "Generative AI Without Guardrails Can Harm Learning: Evidence from High School Mathematics," Proceedings of the National Academy of Sciences 122 (2025), e2422633122. https://doi.org/10.1073/pnas.2422633122. Author-hosted text: https://hamsabastani.github.io/education_llm.pdf. The experiment took place in one Turkish high school. The reported 17 percent reduction concerns the general-purpose-style condition's unassisted exam performance relative to control. The learning-oriented tutor removed the detectable negative effect without establishing an improvement on that exam.

12. Boredom, idle thought, and creativity. Quentin Raffaelli and colleagues, "Creative Minds at Rest: Creative Individuals Are More Associative and Engaged with Their Idle Thoughts," Creativity Research Journal 36, no. 3 (2024): 396-412, https://doi.org/10.1080/10400419.2023.2227477. Colin McDaniel, Assal Habibi, and Jonas Kaplan, "Mind Wandering During Creative Incubation Predicts Increases in Creative Performance in a Writing Task," Scientific Reports 15, article 24629 (2025), https://doi.org/10.1038/s41598-025-09736-y. The chapter preserves associations and the absence of a significant difference among the tested break conditions.

13. Digital distraction in schools. OECD, PISA 2022 Results, Volumes I and II (2023), https://doi.org/10.1787/53f23881-en and https://doi.org/10.1787/a97db61c-en. The chapter distinguishes students' self-reported distraction and associations with performance from causal effects of device use.

14. Technology and education. UNESCO, Global Education Monitoring Report 2023: Technology in Education - A Tool on Whose Terms?, https://gem-report-2023.unesco.org/. The report documents both technology's access benefits and concerns involving distraction, evidence quality, equity, governance, and children's data.

15. Adolescent social media. American Psychological Association, "Health Advisory on Social Media Use in Adolescence" (2023), https://www.apa.org/topics/social-media-internet/health-advisory-adolescent-social-media-use.

16. Generative AI and learning. UNESCO, Guidance for Generative AI in Education and Research (2023), https://www.unesco.org/en/articles/guidance-generative-ai-education-and-research.
This guidance addresses human agency, privacy, inclusion, and educational purpose. The practice suggestions in HUMAN are illustrative applications, not interventions claimed to have been experimentally validated by this report.

17. Global loneliness. WHO Commission on Social Connection, From Loneliness to Social Connection: Charting a Path to Healthier Societies (2025). WHO's accompanying June 30, 2025 news release summarizes the global prevalence estimate and associated health burdens: https://www.who.int/news/item/30-06-2025-social-connection-linked-to-improved-heath-and-reduced-risk-of-early-death.
These estimates are not evidence that a particular relationship intervention will produce a specified health outcome.

18. Social relationships and mortality. Julianne Holt-Lunstad, Timothy B. Smith, and J. Bradley Layton, "Social Relationships and Mortality Risk: A Meta-analytic Review," PLOS Medicine 7, no. 7 (2010), https://pubmed.ncbi.nlm.nih.gov/20668659/. The review included 148 studies and 308,849 participants. The discussion describes an association across prospective studies and does not present the result as proof that any single intervention causes longer life.

19. ELIZA. Joseph Weizenbaum, "ELIZA - A Computer Program for the Study of Natural Language Communication Between Man and Machine," Communications of the ACM 9, no. 1 (1966): 36-45, https://doi.org/10.1145/365153.365168; Computer Power and Human Reason (W. H. Freeman, 1976), p. 259 for the distinction between deciding and choosing. The account of the secretary's private conversation appears in Weizenbaum's introduction, reprinted in The New Media Reader: https://cyborgdigitalculture.files.wordpress.com/2013/09/24-

weizenbaum-03.pdf
(PDF p. 4).

20. The Christmas truce. Imperial War Museums, Lives of the First World War, archived accounts of the Christmas truce, https://livesofthefirstworldwar.iwm.org.uk/story/62266. Encounters varied by location. Reports of football should not be taken to establish one organized match across the front.

21. Political conversation online. Maeve Duggan and Aaron Smith, "The Political Environment on Social Media," Pew Research Center (2016), https://www.pewresearch.org/internet/2016/10/25/the-political-environment-on-social-media/.
The chapter uses the findings directionally and avoids presenting an older survey as a current population estimate.

22. The 1995 Chicago heat wave. Eric Klinenberg, Heat Wave: A Social Autopsy of Disaster in Chicago (University of Chicago Press, 2002). The publisher hosts the author's interview "Dying Alone in the Heat Wave," https://press.uchicago.edu/Misc/Chicago/443213in.html. The disaster's social conditions, not a single cause, inform the chapter.

23. Relationships across the life course. Harvard Study of Adult Development, "History of the Study," https://www.adultdevelopmentstudy.org/grantandglueckstudy. See also Robert Waldinger and Marc Schulz, The Good Life (Simon & Schuster, 2023), the study leaders' account of its findings. The Grant and Glueck cohorts began in different periods; neither is treated as a representative sample of all humanity.

24. Unequal connectivity. International Telecommunication Union, Measuring Digital Development: Facts and Figures 2025, and "Global Number of Internet Users Increases, but Disparities Deepen Key Digital Divides," November 17, 2025.
https://www.itu.int/en/mediacentre/Pages/PR-2025-11-17-facts-and-figures.aspx.
The 6.0 billion online and 2.2 billion offline figures are 2025 estimates. Internet use is not a measure of AI access or effective participation.

25. Language access. NLLB Team, "Scaling Neural Machine Translation to 200 Languages," Nature 630 (2024): 841-846. https://doi.org/10.1038/

s41586-024-07335-x. Language coverage and benchmark performance are not guarantees of equal reliability across languages, dialects, settings, or high-stakes uses. Ethical arguments about participation, permission, and cultural control are the book's arguments, not empirical findings claimed on behalf of this study.

26. Occupational exposure to generative AI. Paweł Gmyrek and colleagues, Generative AI and Jobs: A Refined Global Index of Occupational Exposure, ILO Working Paper 140, May 20, 2025.
https://www.ilo.org/publications/generative-ai-and-jobs-refined-global-index-occupational-exposure.
DOI: https://doi.org/10.54394/HETP0387. Exposure categories estimate tasks potentially affected; they are not observed or forecast job-loss counts. The text distinguishes the highest exposure category from occupations with any exposure.

27. The physical infrastructure of AI. International Energy Agency, Energy and AI (2025), chapter "Energy Demand from AI."
https://www.iea.org/reports/energy-and-ai/energy-demand-from-ai.
The 415 TWh estimate concerns all data centers in 2024, not AI alone. The 945 TWh figure is the report's 2030 base-case projection. No universal per-prompt energy, water, or emissions figure is inferred.

28. Assistive technology and access. WHO, "Assistive Technology," January 2, 2024,
https://www.who.int/news-room/fact-sheets/detail/assistive-technology;
WHO and UNICEF, Global Report on Assistive Technology (2022), https://www.who.int/publications/i/item/9789240049451. Estimates and projections are identified by source date.

29. Speech recognition and disability. Google, "New Ways We're Making Speech Recognition Work for Everyone" (2022),
https://blog.google/company-news/outreach-and-initiatives/accessibility/speech-accessibility-project/.
The word-error improvement is a company-reported research result for adapted systems, not a universal performance guarantee.

30. Communication with an investigational brain-computer interface. UC Davis, "Brain-Computer Interface Allows Man With ALS to 'Speak,'" August 14, 2024.

https://www.ucdavis.edu/news/brain-computer-interface-allows-man-als-speak.
The institutional account describes Casey Harrell's participation, the speech-decoding system, and the associated New England Journal of Medicine study. The manuscript does not invent his dialogue or private thoughts and does not present the experimental system as generally available treatment.

31. Earthrise. NASA, "Earthrise Revisited,"
https://science.nasa.gov/earth/earth-observatory/earthrise-revisited-82693/,
and "NASA Releases New Earthrise Simulation Video,"
https://www.nasa.gov/missions/nasa-releases-new-earthrise-simulation-video/.
William Anders took the color photograph on December 24, 1968, during Apollo 8's fourth lunar orbit.

32. Creativity and collective variety. Anil R. Doshi and Oliver P. Hauser, "Generative AI Enhances Individual Creativity but Reduces the Collective Diversity of Novel Content," Science Advances 10 (2024), eadn5290. https://doi.org/10.1126/sciadv.adn5290. The experiment concerns short-fiction writing with access to generated ideas. Its findings do not establish inevitable effects across all creative work or professional artists.

33. Eleanor W. Dillon, Sonia Jaffe, Nicole Immorlica, and Christopher T. Stanton, "Shifting Work Patterns with Generative AI," NBER Working Paper 33795, May 2025, revised November 2025. https://doi.org/10.3386/w33795. The 66-firm experiment involved 7,137 knowledge workers. The two-hour email reduction concerns users in the second half of the experiment; it is not an estimate for every worker given access.

34. Flood forecasting. Grey Nearing and colleagues, "Global Prediction of Extreme Floods in Ungauged Watersheds," Nature 627 (2024): 559-563. https://doi.org/10.1038/s41586-024-07145-1. Author preprint: "AI Increases Global Access to Reliable Flood Forecasts," version 4 (2023), https://arxiv.org/abs/2307.16104. The manuscript's claims concern forecasting reliability and deployment described in the research. The household evacuation scenes are hypothetical and are not reported outcomes or estimates of lives saved.

www.ingramcontent.com/pod-product-compliance
Lightning Source LLC
LaVergne TN
LVHW010719061126
851857LV00014B/1251
* 9 7 9 8 9 9 7 3 0 5 0 7 9 *